Bringing Antiracism into Focus

This guide introduces applied antiracist developmental science and developmental frameworks that have been comprehensively integrated with antiracist principles. It underscores the importance of viewing child and adolescent development-related work through an antiracist lens from the outset, examining how systemic racism, implicit bias, and critical consciousness shape human development, and emphasizes the need to cultivate an antiracist developmental perspective to promote equity in professional settings.

Anchored in the foundational bioecological model, this book extends to additional frameworks such as the Racism + Resilience + Resistance Integrative Study of Childhood Ecosystem (R³ISE), the Integrative Model of Ethnic Minority Development, the Multicontextual Model for Diverse Learning Environments, and the Phenomenological Variant of Ecological Systems Theory (PVEST). These frameworks are adapted to confront racism and support antiracist practices.

Targeted discussions in dedicated chapters cover fields such as psychology, PK-12 education, higher education, and allied health. This book bridges theory and practice through case studies, practical examples, and reflective activities, demonstrating how to incorporate antiracist strategies into daily professional practice. It also delves into how community assets can be protective and mitigate the effects of racism, guiding professionals to recognize and leverage these strengths effectively.

This resource is designed for students, pre-professionals, and early-career professionals in child and adolescent development committed to incorporating antiracist practices into their work. It serves as both an introductory overview and a practical manual for applying developmental principles with an emphasis on reflection and praxis.

Alicia Herrera is Assistant Professor of Child and Adolescent Development in the College of Education at California State University, Sacramento, USA. Her research examines ethnic-racial identity development within educational contexts, focusing on how educators understand their mediating roles in these processes. As a qualitative researcher and teacher educator, she explores positionality, racial literacy, and the development of critical consciousness in professional settings. Her work supports antiracist developmental theory in practice.

Kevin Ferreira van Leer is Assistant Professor of Human Development and Family Sciences at the University of Connecticut. As an action researcher, he examines the sociocultural and policy contexts that promote positive development and liberation for Latine immigrants and their families. He largely utilizes community-engaged research, collaborating directly with immigrant communities to develop research projects around their concerns, build their capacity to conduct research themselves, and share findings for positive change.

Samantha Blackburn is Director of the Community Engagement Center at California State University, Sacramento. She received her PhD in Nursing Science and Health-Care Leadership from the University of California, Davis Betty Irene Moore School of Nursing. Her current research interests are school health program administration, interdisciplinary education, and experiential learning.

Applying Child and Adolescent Development in the Professions Series
Kimberly A. Gordon Biddle
*Emeritus Professor of Child and Adolescent Development,
Sacramento State, California, USA*

The field of Child and Adolescent Development is being recognized and legitimized more and more as good preparation for a variety of careers in various fields, such as psychology, education, allied health, non-profits, and social work. As more theories are created and research is conducted, more attention and recognition are given to the field of Child and Adolescent Development.

This series will take the core and current topics in the field of Child and Adolescent Development, define these topics, describe these topics as they develop in children from infancy to age 25 or describe how the topic impacts children from infancy to age 25, and then apply them to careers in five main fields, psychology, education, allied health, non-profits, and social work. Various application strategies and techniques will be shared. The core topics addressed in this series of books are attachment, motivation, social and emotional competence, executive function, and multilingual and multicultural development. The current niche topics represented in the series are these; transformative frames for anti-racism, socio-cultural deprivation, and growth mindset for transformative thinking. The writing level is to be accessible and engaging for students in high school and the first or second year of college. However, the information may be useful for graduate students, too. These books are excellent for early, mid, and late career professionals, too. Employee training and professional development can be enriched with the books of this series.

It is the intention of the book authors that our books are helpful to all people who work with and care for children. Indeed, the 8 books of the Applying Child and Adolescent Development in the Professions Series move the field forward.

Dr. Kimberly A. Gordon Biddle spent over 30 years working full-time in the field of Child and Adolescent Development, with 2 years as a Research Analyst and 28 plus years as a College Professor. Currently, she is an Emeritus Professor of Child and Adolescent Development from Sacramento State in California. Her BA is in Psychology and Music from the University of Redlands. Her EdS is in Program Evaluation and her PhD is in Child and Adolescent Development. Both of her advanced degrees are from Stanford University.

Over her career she has been an American Psychological Association MFP fellow. She has authored or co-authored over 20 articles and some book chapters. She has presented or co-presented over 40 presentations. Before being the overall editor of this series she had co-authored or co-edited 4 textbooks. She has obtained approximately $1,000,000 in grants. Her research and teaching areas of expertise include motivation, academic resilience, social and emotional development, and the education and socialization of marginalized groups. She also has some expertise in field work placement and coordination and policies concerning children and families. Her career efforts have been rewarded. For example, she has received Outstanding Teaching and Service Awards from Sacramento State. She also won a Stanford Graduate School of Education Award for Excellence in Education in 2018 and a Career Award from the University of Redlands in 2019.

She is thrilled that Editor Helen Pritt at Routledge asked her to be the lead editor of this book series and she has enjoyed nurturing the series into life. She is happy to now be working with editor Molly Selby. This series is near and dear to her heart and she is honored to edit it and co-author one of the books. She firmly believes that this book series will move the field of Child and Adolescent Development forward. Core concepts of the field and current topics of the field are explored and applied in an engaging manner. Dr. Biddle firmly believes that knowledge of the field of Child and Adolescent Development can assist so many people, whether they are family members of children or are in careers working with children. This series aims to assist those in a wide range of careers who work with children. Those aims are met and surpassed in this series in the opinion of Dr. Biddle. It is her hope that this series is used with students in secondary, undergraduate, and graduate education settings in addition to adults in the fields of education, psychology, social work, allied health, and non-profit organizations. This series is the jewel in Dr. Biddle's career crown. She hopes it shines brightly.

Inspiring Motivation in Children and Youth
How to Nurture Environments for Learning
David A. Bergin

Promoting Regulation and Flexibility in Thinking
Development of Executive Function
Kristen M. Weede Alexander and Karen M. Davis O'Hara

From Cultural Deprivation to Cultural Security
Tackling Socio-Cultural Deprivation with Children and Young People
Dale Allender and Arya Allender-West

Social and Emotional Development in Children through Emerging Adults
A Guide for Professionals
Kimberly A. Gordon Biddle and Christi Bergin

Bringing Antiracism into Focus
Using Transformative Lenses to Reframe Professional Practice
Alicia Herrera, Kevin Ferreira van Leer, and Samantha Blackburn

Enhancing Multilingual Development
A Guide for Professionals
Nadeen T. Ruiz and Andrea García

For more information about this series, please visit: www.routledge.com/Applying-Child-and-Adolescent-Development-in-the-Professions-Series/book-series/ACADP

Bringing Antiracism into Focus

Using Transformative Lenses to Reframe Professional Practice

Alicia Herrera, Kevin Ferreira van Leer and Samantha Blackburn

NEW YORK AND LONDON

Designed cover image: © Praveenkumar Palanichamy via Getty Images

First published 2025
by Routledge
605 Third Avenue, New York, NY 10158

and by Routledge
4 Park Square, Milton Park, Abingdon, Oxon OX14 4RN

Routledge is an imprint of the Taylor & Francis Group, an informa business

© 2025 Alicia Herrera, Kevin Ferreira van Leer and Samantha Blackburn

The right of Alicia Herrera, Kevin Ferreira van Leer and Samantha Blackburn to be identified as authors of this work has been asserted in accordance with sections 77 and 78 of the Copyright, Designs and Patents Act 1988.

All rights reserved. No part of this book may be reprinted or reproduced or utilised in any form or by any electronic, mechanical, or other means, now known or hereafter invented, including photocopying and recording, or in any information storage or retrieval system, without permission in writing from the publishers.

Trademark notice: Product or corporate names may be trademarks or registered trademarks, and are used only for identification and explanation without intent to infringe.

ISBN: 978-1-032-44840-4 (hbk)
ISBN: 978-1-032-44841-1 (pbk)
ISBN: 978-1-003-37417-6 (ebk)

DOI: 10.4324/9781003374176

Typeset in Times New Roman
by codeMantra

To Brad, for your steadfast support, and to Oz, whose curiosity and sense of justice inspire me.

— AH

To my late father, Bob Blackburn, whose commitment to radical antiracism and educational reform inspires me every day.

— SB

To Kyle, my life partner in making good trouble, and Greyson who continually inspires me to reimagine the lenses in which I read the world.

— KF

Contents

List of Illustrations	xv
Foreword	xvii

Introduction   1
Welcome 1
Who Should Read This Book? 1
How to Navigate This Book 2
Key Features of Chapters 2–5 2
Let's Begin 3

1   Foundations: Antiracist Developmental Frameworks and Models   4
Introduction 4
Key Definitions and Frameworks 6
Becoming an Antiracist Professional 17
Chapter Summaries 26
Critical Questions 27
References 28

2   Examining and Resisting Racism through Psychology   32
Introduction 32
Theories to Examine and Resist Racism in Psychology 33
Critical Issues and Practices 38
Developing an Antiracist Professional Identity within Psychology 45
Reflect and Practice Activities 50
Chapter Summary 52
Recommended Resources 53
References 53

3 Antiracist Developmental Teaching in PK-12 Education   58
Introduction 58
Foundations of Teacher Identity 60
Extending Vygotsky's Zone of Proximal Development 63
The White Zones of Proximal Development 65
Establishing a Critical Reflective Practice 67
*Applying Antiracist Developmental Frameworks
    in PK-12 Contexts 72*
Practical Example: A Tale of Two Classrooms 76
Reflect and Practice Activities 80
Chapter Summary 83
Recommended Resources 83
References 84

4 An Antiracist Developmental View of Higher Education   87
Introduction 87
An Ecological Model for Higher Education 88
*From Bronfenbrenner to the MMDLE: Bridging
    Understanding 89*
*Affirming and Sustaining Student Identity in Higher
    Education 92*
*Intersectionality and Critical Consciousness
    in Student Development 93*
Antiracism and Development 95
Centering Relationships and Emotional Support 96
Engaging in Advocacy 97
*Developmentally Informed Mentorship and Support
    Systems 97*
Critical Issues and Considerations 99
Antiracist Professional Identity Development 104
Reflect and Practice Activities 105
Chapter Summary 109
Recommended Resources 109
References 110

5 Antiracist Approaches for Allied Health Professionals   113
Introduction 113
*Applying Key Concepts and Theoretical Frameworks to
    Health 115*

Critical Issues and Practices 118
Strategies for Addressing Racism 120
Developing an Antiracist Health Professional Identity 127
Reflect and Practice Activities 129
Chapter Summary 132
Recommended Resources 133
References 133

Index *137*

Illustrations

Figures

1.1 The Bioecological Model Serves as a Classic Example of an Ecological Model. Created by Megan R Waechter-McMillan, used with permission   11
3.1 Traditional Zone of Proximal Development   64
3.2 Whites Zone of Proximal Development   66

Boxes

1.1 Using Process-Person-Context-Time to Examine Racism   13
1.2 Early Career Steps for Developing an Antiracist Lens in Your Profession   19
1.3 Antiracist Praxis Model   23
2.1 Implementing Healing Justice Practices: A Case Study on the Alaska Native Cultural Identity Project (CIP)   41
2.2 Integrating Liberation and Counseling Psychology: A Case Study of Group Workshops Deconstructing Gender-based Violence and Taking Action with Women of Burma   47
5.1 Youth Risk Behavior Surveillance System   122

Tables

2.1 Sample matrix to explore racial/ethnic breakdown of samples in empirical articles around a topic of interest   51

Foreword

The field of Child and Adolescent Development is in its infant stages of development, but it is steadily maturing. It is time for it to be recognized and legitimized. As the theorizing and conduction of research in the field become more solid, complex, and applicable to life, recognition comes that the field is for people in a variety of professions. The traditional education and psychology fields are enriched with the knowledge obtained from the field of Child and Adolescent Development. Additionally, allied health, social work, and non-profit fields are improved with knowledge of how to apply Child and Adolescent Development in the workplace setting. Everyone who works with or cares for children from birth to 25 years will benefit from reading and applying the information from the books in this series.

Collectively, the authors have created books rich with foundational information and application techniques and strategies. Thematic boxes of interviews, case studies, and research and theory into practice run throughout all the books. These books help to answer some of the most important questions concerning children and their development. All who love and care about children should read every book in the series.

I am quite happy to welcome this innovative and thoughtful textbook into the Applying Child and Adolescent Development in the Professions Series. Antiracism is still an important topic in Child and Adolescent Development today. This group of authors have done a wonderful job of presenting the importance and applicability of antiracism. The title of their textbook truly exemplifies the contents, *Bringing Antiracism into Focus: Using Transformative Lenses to Reframe Professional Practice*. This group of authors have also created a new theoretical model that adds to the Child and Adolescent Development Literature and Practice. The textbook includes pertinent frameworks, theories concerning racism, case studies, and critical questions. This book is an excellent addition to the bookshelves of many professionals in a variety of fields, because the impact of racism on children is deep and consequential.

Dr. Kimberly A. Gordon Biddle

Introduction

Welcome

You have opened this book and are most likely wondering what to expect. To be clear from the start, the contents within these pages will either resonate with you…or will not. That is the nature of this kind of work. So, we would like to be transparent and build trust by sharing our intent as the authors of this book from the very beginning.

The United States is, as it often seems to be, entering an era of significant change. At the time of writing, the 2024 presidential election had just been decided, and the nation was once again grappling with vast differences in interpretations of what the identity of the United States is and should become. The new presidential administration has initiated a dismantling of widely accepted approaches to diversity, equity, and inclusion across society. We, the authors, have chosen to focus on certain aspects of development and antiracism in this book that we expect to be enduring, while acknowledging the fast-paced nature of our times and recognizing that the near future will inevitably bring new language, topics, and changes that this book cannot anticipate.

Who Should Read This Book?

This book is written for students and early-career professionals, who intend to work with children and families and want to *apply both a developmental and an antiracist lens to their work*. We write with the understanding that you, the reader, are already "on board," at least in spirit, with the concept of antiracism. In other words, this book is not intended to persuade but to supplement current developmental literature. As professors in the field, we aim to bridge the gap between contemporary literature on antiracism and the general developmental texts often relied upon in university courses to prepare professionals.

This book includes individual chapters that focus on specific developmental fields, such as psychology, PK-12 education, higher education, and allied health. Each chapter is valuable for all readers, even those not planning to enter a particular field, as chapters offer different antiracist extensions to traditional frameworks in each field. Instead of reinforcing the established structures and practices commonly found in traditional textbooks, these extensions encourage a critical approach to understanding and applying developmental knowledge. Through these frameworks, you will identify and challenge ways of thinking and doing that perpetuate inequity, ultimately helping you in your plans to reshape any field you enter with a more equitable, justice-centered perspective on human development.

How to Navigate This Book

The book's structure is both developmental and professions-specific, with each chapter building on the last to deepen your understanding of antiracist principles and practices within the field:

Chapter 1: Read this first. This chapter serves as an introduction to key antiracist developmental frameworks and provides the groundwork for the more specialized, field-specific discussions that follow. It introduces early career steps for developing an antiracist lens as you enter your profession. Additionally, it introduces an Antiracist Praxis Model to guide you in applying antiracism in everyday career situations. These steps and this model support understanding and applying antiracist approaches that strengthen and deepen practice in developmental fields.

Chapters 2–5: Each chapter focuses on a distinct developmental profession – psychology, PK-12 education, higher education, and allied health – exploring unique challenges and opportunities for antiracist work within each context. These chapters provide field-specific insights, relevant overviews, and structured opportunities for reflection and practice.

Interconnected Principles: You might feel compelled to read only those chapters specific to your intended developmental professional – but don't do it! As you progress through the book, you'll see how the antiracist approaches connect across developmental contexts, building a comprehensive understanding of how these concepts apply within and across professional environments.

Key Features of Chapters 2–5

Each chapter offers unique antiracist approaches and discussions about developmental science, highlighting salient themes specific to each profession. These elements challenge established practices and encourage an equity-focused approach to understanding and applying developmental knowledge. In addition to these core components, each chapter will include the following:

Practical Examples: Some chapters include a practical example, presented as a vignette, that illustrates an issue specific to the field. You will be guided through an analysis of these examples using antiracist developmental concepts.

Case Studies: Each chapter contains a case study activity, providing you with the opportunity to practice applying antiracist strategies to developmental frameworks within a professional setting.

Critical Questions: Reflection and discussion prompts at the end of each chapter encourage critical thinking, helping you connect theoretical insights to practical applications, and deepen engagement with the material.

Resources: Each chapter provides a list of recommended books, articles, and other resources to support continued exploration of antiracist practices within developmental fields.

Additional Exercises: Chapters 2–5 feature other various profession-specific exercises designed to help you further apply the frameworks to analyze systemic racism within organizations and communities, and examine power structures, resource allocation, and institutional practices. You will gain experience practicing the act of recognizing and leveraging existing strengths, cultural knowledge, support networks, and antiracist efforts within your communities or organizations, shifting the focus from deficits to leveraging available assets and resources for fostering positive change.

Let's Begin

We sincerely hope that the developmental learning (and unlearning) prompted by this book will serve you well as you approach your work with children and adolescents in the world. Thank you for your willingness to engage with this content and for taking these steps to integrate an antiracist lens into your professional practice.

Chapter 1

Foundations
Antiracist Developmental Frameworks and Models

Introduction

As university professors, we spend countless hours guiding students as they prepare for their dream careers in child and adolescent development. We also mentor early-career professionals who are learning on the job, facing the real-world complexities of their fields. In both cases, we've seen firsthand the "traps, gaps, and lags" between cutting-edge developmental science, what's taught in universities, and what's actually practiced in the workplace. This disconnect is hardly surprising. New research takes time to filter from publication to classroom, and educators often rely on what they themselves were taught, even when it's outdated. Familiar texts are used when there's no time to explore newer materials, and workplace practices shift slowly, further compounding the issue. Generational divides in thinking between newcomers and seasoned professionals deepen this disconnect. Given these realities, it's no wonder students and professionals alike may miss out on the latest insights in their field.

And then there is racism. As a *multidimensional system of oppression and exclusion*, racism is deeply embedded in the foundation of the United States (Jones, 2000). Racism functions as a hierarchy of power and privilege, structured to maintain dominance while resisting examination (Delgado & Stefancic, 2017; Iruka et al., 2022). Although it permeates every aspect of society, many early-career professionals in child and adolescent development continue to *report limited exposure to antiracist perspectives in developmental theory or practice.* They often cite both university and professional learning experiences that rendered non-dominant perspectives, if not fully invisible, then frequently overlooked, silenced, or dismissed (Syed et al., 2022).

Developmental science highlights the urgent need to address systemic racism in child and adolescent fields, as it is one of the most harmful and trauma-inducing factors affecting children's health and development in the United States (Iruka et al., 2022; Saleem et al., 2020; Trent et al., 2019). *Systemic racism permeates nearly every part of society* and has a significant impact on professions related to child development, including education and healthcare (Gee et al.,

DOI: 10.4324/9781003374176-2

2012; Iruka et al., 2022). It is essential that we recognize that every person's individual professional practice is part of larger social structures and can work to perpetuate or dismantle racism. We do not exist in a vacuum.

But where to begin thinking about all of this? And when? The answer is, if you are reading this book, to start now, at the very beginning of your career, *by framing your professional thinking through an antiracist lens*. Starting early is crucial, as how you begin to think about your work shapes patterns: patterns of thinking, being, and action. This is the time when you are learning the essence of your profession.

For instance, you may be enrolled in fieldwork courses where you gain firsthand experience *connecting theory-to-practice*, learning through doing, or observing the modeling of a mentor or supervisor at a placement. However, if you do not want to thoughtlessly replicate and reinforce the values, practices, and behaviors that came before you, how do you *critically question what you are seeing and doing*, especially when you are new to the field and eager to learn from experienced professionals? This is the balancing act and the critical challenge: to thoughtfully sift through what you observe and experience in real time and make sense of it. By actively engaging with the **Early Career Steps for Developing an Antiracist Lens in Your Profession** and **Antiracist Praxis Model** presented below as well as applying **antiracist developmental frameworks**, you can act with intentionality, recognize the reification of racist structures, disrupt harmful norms, and shift perspectives in your practice.

This book is specifically written to encourage learning, critical thinking, and conversations that we hope will soon become more commonplace among pre-professionals and early-career professionals. Familiarity with antiracist developmental frameworks from the beginning can help integrate antiracism into your work as an everyday, essential element. By embedding antiracist developmental science in your thinking and addressing the necessary "unlearning," you gain the agency needed to shape your professional identity and practice (Leonardo & Manning, 2017).

For this reason, the intended audience of this book are those preparing for their careers and also those who are in the early stages of their professional journey. This includes those seeking degrees in child and adolescent development, human development and family studies, developmental psychology, education and related fields, as well as those engaging in professional development. It is written for any individuals who aspire to work with children, adolescents, and families while applying a developmental and antiracist lens to their practice and wish to have some guided experiences in doing so. Our goal is to enhance current developmental literature and bridge the gap between recent advancements in developmental science and the more traditional content taught in university settings. An important detail: although some content in this book may read as "persuasive" at times, it is important to note that the purpose of this book is not to *convince* but to provide a *foundation* for understanding and applying antiracist principles. This distinction is essential in recognizing the book's intent.

Embracing antiracist practices can lead to profound changes that extend beyond individual benefits and enrich the field as a whole. The pervasive impact of systemic racism is evident, well-documented, and will be explored in various areas in this book. To understand the scale and impact of systemic racism, consider these statistics and examples:

Education: Black and Latine students are disproportionately disciplined compared to their White peers, leading to long-term negative effects, such as the "school-to-prison pipeline" (Lindsay & Hart, 2017; US Department of Education Office of Civil Rights, 2014).

Allied Health: Long-term exposure to structural racism and discrimination acts as a chronic stressor that impacts individuals on multiple levels, contributing to negative birth outcomes and racial disparities in maternal mortality (Alhusen et al., 2016; Collier & Molina, 2019).

Counseling: Clinical practitioners with limited experience in cross-racial work may attribute minoritized-race survivors' outcomes to individual failings rather than recognizing the broader social determinants impacting their circumstances, thereby reinforcing stigma and hindering effective support (Parenteau et al., 2023).

The brief examples above serve as starting points for appreciating the importance of engaging with this book and the deep commitment antiracist developmental practice demands. This work requires *making connections between the personal and the systemic*, and being willing to engage in individual reflection within a broader societal context. This commitment involves personal growth and the ongoing challenge of *recognizing and addressing biases*, advocating for equitable policies, and supporting others in their antiracist efforts. It means developing the skills needed to understand the current environment and taking responsibility for creating spaces where everyone can thrive.

Adopting antiracist practices extends beyond meeting compliance standards or checking off a "competence" box; it is about transforming how one approaches their work and interacts with others. Antiracism necessitates *continuous self-reflection and education*. Incorporating these principles early, during the foundational stages of professional development, positions individuals to effectively challenge and dismantle structures that sustain racism within their **sphere of influence**. Committing to antiracist practice is essential for fostering the well-being of the communities served and for upholding the integrity and impact of one's professional work.

Key Definitions and Frameworks

Scholars in child and adolescent development draw from a variety of definitions and frameworks to inform their antiracist practice. Below we outline some key definitions and frameworks related to antiracism. Becoming familiar with these concepts is a first step toward antiracist practice.

While the following definitions and frameworks reflect the current state of our field, they are not an exhaustive list. Additionally, we recognize that these definitions may change over time. Thus, we encourage professionals to seek out those that are commonly used in their profession and keep up to date of changes in the field.

Talking through Definitions

Before delving into antiracist practices, it is important to start with a clear understanding of key terms related to racism. Familiarity with these definitions helps us identify how racism manifests in our personal and professional lives, discuss it with others, and take actionable steps to address it.

First, we must acknowledge that **race** is a **socially constructed concept** (Smedley & Smedley, 2005). This means that race does not have a biological basis but is a classification system that societies have created based on physical attributes, such as hair texture or skin color (Iruka et al., 2022). The definition and categorization of racial groups have varied throughout history and across different societies. Despite its social construction, race has *significant real-world consequences*. Racial categories shape people's experiences, access to resources, and overall outcomes in life. These outcomes are not due to inherent differences among racial groups but are the result of **systemic racism** (Gaylord-Harden et al., 2020; Seaton, 2020; Tai et al., 2021).

In broadest terms, **racism** can be defined as a system of advantage based on race, which benefits White people and creates barriers to success and well-being for people of color (Bonilla-Silva, 2017). This system operates at various levels, from individual interactions to structural policies and practices that sustain racial hierarchies. Understanding that racism is *systemic* rather than just limited to individual acts of prejudice helps us recognize how deeply ingrained it is in society.

The impacts of racism can be seen across many aspects of life, such as education, healthcare, employment, and housing. For instance, disparities in educational opportunities and outcomes often correlate with race, but these *disparities are not due to an inherent characteristic of any racial group*. Instead, they stem from discriminatory policies and practices that disproportionately affect marginalized communities (Gaylord-Harden et al., 2020).

The ultimate goal of recognizing these definitions is to make moves toward **racial equity**, which means creating conditions where race no longer predicts one's success or well-being in society. Racial equity involves proactive measures to address and dismantle systems of racism, ensuring fair treatment, access, and opportunities for all people, regardless of their racial background (Gorski, 2016). Achieving racial equity *requires acknowledging existing systemic inequalities and working actively to create systems-level changes* that promote justice and fairness. By understanding the foundational concepts of race, racism, justice, and racial equity, we can better engage in meaningful antiracist practice. This practice involves not only recognizing and addressing overt acts of racism but also examining how policies, practices, and biases perpetuate **systemic inequities**. In short, this practice requires one to be racially literate.

Understanding and developing **racial literacy** is foundational for engaging in meaningful discussions about race and racism. Racial literacy refers to the ability to recognize, name, and critically engage with issues of race and racism, using precise and informed language. In the United States, conversations about race are often avoided due to social taboos or efforts to adopt a "colorblind" perspective, which can lead to **colorblind racism**. This approach downplays or ignores the importance of race and systemic factors, maintaining the status quo and contributing to ongoing inequities (Bonilla-Silva, 2015; Hochschild, 1996; Syed, 2016). Instead of acknowledging the role that race plays in shaping societal outcomes, colorblind racism provides race-neutral explanations for race-related issues, ultimately reinforcing racial disparities. We imagine that you may have heard the phrase, "I don't see color," spoken by a well-meaning person. The problem is that you cannot fight racism if you do not acknowledge that race and racism exist in the first place. For professionals working in fields related to child and adolescent development, having basic racial literacy is essential for critical thinking.

Developing racial literacy also means understanding and using terminology accurately. Words like *race*, *ethnicity*, *culture*, and *nationality* are often used loosely and interchangeably in the field, leading to confusion and missed opportunities for meaningful engagement. Additionally, vague terms like "diverse" are sometimes used as a proxy to avoid directly addressing race, which further obscures discussions about racism. Outdated terms such as "Caucasian" are often used as an intended euphemism by people who may feel uncomfortable saying the word "White." This imprecision with language can hinder the ability to fully confront systemic issues. This goes beyond simply being particular or insisting on politically correct terminology: having a strong grasp of definitions and language related to racism is an essential step for anyone committed to antiracist work for many reasons. For example, in Chapters 2–6, you will see how this imprecision manifests in research and practice that attribute developmental differences to presumed deficiencies within marginalized groups, without considering systemic influences such as socioeconomic conditions or access to resources (Cauce et al., 1998; Gjerde, 2004; Helms et al., 2005). It is crucial to know what you intend to say and to express it clearly. The consequences are real and affect real people.

We will go over many profession-specific details around racism in Chapters 2–5, but in general, **racism**, as defined in this book, follows Jones' (2002) framework, which identifies three interconnected levels: personally mediated, institutionalized, and internalized.

- **Personally mediated racism** involves individual acts of discrimination or prejudice based on race. These acts, whether intentional or unconscious,

manifest in daily interactions and include biased treatment, microaggressions, or discriminatory practices in professional settings. Such racism reinforces stereotypes and perpetuates power imbalances. This is what people most typically think of when they think of "racist."
- **Institutionalized racism** encompasses the broader structures in society, including laws, policies, and institutional practices that create and sustain racial inequities. This type of racism determines access to resources and opportunities, embedding disparities in systems such as education, healthcare, housing, and the criminal justice system. Also known as *systemic* or *structural* racism, it is often less visible and harder to address because it is built into the fabric of societal norms and practices.
- **Internalized racism** refers to the internalization of negative beliefs and stereotypes about one's own racial group(s), impacting self-perception and worth. This affects individuals of all racial backgrounds and leads to conscious or unconscious comparisons to dominant cultural standards. For instance, someone with physical traits commonly associated with a minoritized group, such as 4C hair type or skin with higher concentrations of melanin, may view these features as undesirable due to persistent cultural messaging that devalues them. Internalized racism influences behavior, self-esteem, and mental health, creating cycles of disadvantage.

With these definitions in mind, we turn to antiracism. **Antiracism**, as articulated by Kendi (2019), is an active process that involves recognizing and addressing racism in all its forms, both historically and in current practice. It challenges narratives that suggest differing self-worth among racial groups, examines how power perpetuates inequities, and supports policies that dismantle systemic disparities (Kendi, 2019; People's Institute for Survival and Beyond, 2025). Antiracism is not a static achievement but *a cycle of learning, reflection, and action*. This book will explore what antiracism looks like in professional practice and, specifically, how it can guide equitable approaches in child and adolescent development.

It is important to recognize that racism is not the only form of oppression affecting individuals. People can experience intersecting forms of discrimination based on various aspects of their identity, such as socioeconomic status, gender, ability, sexual orientation, and age. **Intersectionality**, a concept developed by Crenshaw (1991), offers a way to examine how these different systems of oppression overlap and influence people's experiences. This framework was shaped by the contributions of Black feminists, women of color, and queer scholars who critiqued approaches that focused on single identities and failed to address the complexity of systemic inequality (Collins, 2019; Combahee River Collective, 1977/1983; Crenshaw, 1991). For instance, the challenges faced by a Latina woman may not be the same as those faced by a Latino man or a queer Latina woman, as *different aspects of identity interact to create unique experiences of discrimination.* Understanding intersectionality enables professionals to grasp how overlapping systems of power impact individuals and groups (Syed et al., 2018). Although we center and focus on racism and antiracism in this book, these constructs can often intersect with other forms of oppression.

Frameworks for Understanding Development and Racism

As you begin thinking about your potential future career working with child and adolescent development, it is useful to begin familiarizing yourself with the ways in which developmental scientists think about racism and development. The field of child and adolescent development provides a unique perspective into thinking about the ways that racism impacts individuals over the life course.

Ecological theories are widely used to consider the ways in which individuals develop within multiple settings of their environment. The **bioecological model** (Bronfenbrenner & Morris, 2006) is the most widely used framework within the field and can help us to understand ecological models, in general, and be used as a springboard to *begin* our thinking about the ways that racism may shape the development of children and adolescents, *though it does not explicitly address race, racism, and inequity by design*. However, this model does emphasize the role of processes in understanding how the interaction between an individual and their environment influences development in general and makes space for a general consideration of context. This means that if we want to consider racism with this model, we can do so. Depending on your future career, there may be specific proximal processes that are particularly significant within the environments in which you work and, by developing confidence with the bioecological model, you can use any number of ecological theories and models to organize your thinking.

Let's use the bioecological model as our example to detail the ways that ecological models can capture a good view of systemic racism. The **bioecological model** specifically encourages us to focus on **processes** between an individual and their context, emphasizing interactions between the person and their environment that become increasingly complex over time. For professionals in education, these processes might include student-teacher interactions, while for those in social work could involve client-caseworker relationships or community-based interventions. To fully understand how these processes influence development, the model asks us to consider **person**, **context**, and **time**, in addition to the **process** itself (Figure 1.1).

Starting with the **person**, the model prompts us to examine what the individual brings to their environment and how they elicit responses from it. This includes characteristics that influence interactions, such as resources related to social position (e.g., gender, age), personality traits (e.g., temperament), or cognitive factors (e.g., experience, knowledge). These characteristics shape how

Foundations: Antiracist Developmental Frameworks and Models 11

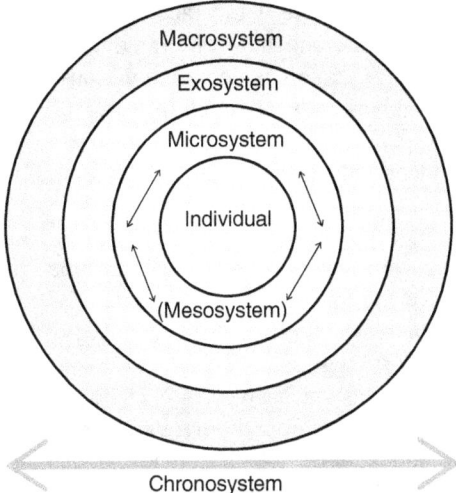

Figure 1.1 The Bioecological Model Serves as a Classic Example of an Ecological Model. Created by Megan R Waechter-McMillan, used with permission.

others interact with the individual and how the individual engages with their environment.

Next, the model discusses the role of **context**, or the different levels of the environment. In the bioecological model, these are often depicted as nested systems: microsystem, mesosystem, exosystem, and macrosystem. The **microsystem** consists of the immediate environments where direct interactions occur, such as family, school, peer groups, and healthcare settings. The **mesosystem** refers to the interactions between different microsystems, such as the relationship between a child's school and home. The **exosystem** encompasses environments that do not directly involve the individual but still have an indirect impact on their development, such as parental workplace policies or government regulations.

The **macrosystem** represents the larger cultural and ideological context that shapes the underlying structures of all the other systems. Recognizing the role of different environments, some directly experienced and others more removed, is crucial for understanding how a person interacts with and is influenced by their surroundings.

Lastly, the model highlights the importance of **time**, which involves considering when processes occur in an individual's life, how frequently they happen, and the length of time over which they unfold. It also considers the broader historical period in which these processes take place, adding another layer to how development is shaped.

To illustrate how this model can help us understand how racism impacts development, consider the *process* of **ethnic-racial socialization**. This refers to the messages children receive about race and ethnicity, which can shape their understanding of race and how they navigate racism (Hughes et al., 2006). Ethnic-racial socialization can occur in various *contexts*, such as families, schools, and neighborhoods, although research often focuses on the family microsystem.

Scholars have identified several types of messages within ethnic-racial socialization:

1 **Cultural socialization**, which promotes cultural pride by teaching children about their heritage and traditions;
2 **Preparation for bias**, which raises awareness about potential discrimination and provides coping strategies;
3 **Promotion of mistrust**, which involves encouraging caution or distrust in interactions with individuals from different racial or ethnic backgrounds; and
4 **Egalitarianism and silence**, which emphasizes individual traits, such as work ethic, over racial or ethnic identity.

Children may receive a combination of these messages, with some occurring more frequently than others. These messages may also differ across *contexts*. For example, while a child might learn about culturally relevant music and stories and be encouraged to take pride in their heritage within the family (cultural socialization), school messages may focus on individual achievement and hard work (egalitarianism and silence). Research has shown that positive cultural socialization can buffer the negative effects of discrimination for youth of color (Yosso, 2005). Additionally, adolescents who receive preparation for bias messages often demonstrate more effective coping strategies when facing interpersonal discrimination (Bowers et al., 2021).

The bioecological model also encourages us to consider the **timing** of these processes, for instance, how often and at what points in a child's development these messages are conveyed. Some families proactively incorporate these messages into daily life, while others address them reactively in response to specific events.

The model further prompts us to examine how individual characteristics affect these processes. For example, researchers have found that the content and frequency of ethnic-racial socialization messages can vary by child gender and age, with older youth of color more likely to receive preparation for bias and promotion of mistrust messages. Parental characteristics also play a role; parents with higher levels of education are more likely to engage in cultural socialization and preparation for bias (Wang et al., 2020).

In summary, research on ethnic-racial socialization demonstrates how the bioecological model's emphasis on person, process, context, and time can deepen our understanding of the ways racism impacts development.

> **Box 1.1 Using Process-Person-Context-Time to Examine Racism**
>
> A process-person-context-time understanding of the bioecological model prepares us with some central questions we can use to understand how racism may appear in our workplaces as well as influence the development of those that we work with:
>
> - **Process:** What are the essential processes, or complex interactions unfolding over time, that are going on and shaping their development? How might these processes be shaped by racism?
> - **Person:** What are the dispositions, resources, and demands that a person brings to the situation? Are specific dispositions, resources, and demands influenced by race/ethnicity and racism?
> - **Context:** How is racism playing out in the immediate context? How does the relationship between the immediate contexts (e.g., school and home; health clinic and school) illustrate how racism may influence development? What are the indirect contexts that might shape how racism influences development? How do larger beliefs about race, racism, and systems of oppression shape development?
> - **Time:** How often are these processes happening? How does our historical period tell us about how we understand racism (e.g., Jim Crow era racism compared to Systems of Mass Incarceration)? Does developmental timing matter?

There are multiple resources that communities of color may draw on that have been documented to buffer the impacts of racism. Yosso's (2005) concept of **community cultural wealth** highlights a variety of knowledge and resources cultivated by these communities to navigate and resist systemic oppression. These resources include practices and strengths developed within families, social networks, and communities that enable them to confront racism. This wealth includes ways of communicating, envisioning the future, and passing down cultural knowledge that supports resilience and the ability to imagine a future beyond the limitations imposed by current systems of oppression.

The framework identifies several forms of cultural capital: **aspirational, navigational, social, linguistic, familial, and resistant**. Aspirational capital reflects hope and the ability to maintain dreams for the future, even in the face of systemic barriers. Navigational capital refers to the skills and strategies required to move through environments not designed to support marginalized groups. Social capital encompasses the networks of support and relationships that provide opportunities and emotional resources. Linguistic capital includes the diverse communication skills developed through multilingualism and non-dominant forms of expression. Familial capital involves the cultural knowledge and collective memory shared within families that emphasize community and cultural identity. Resistant capital embodies the practices and knowledge that have been developed to challenge and push back against inequities.

These forms of community cultural wealth can act as **protective factors** against the negative effects of systemic racism. Understanding and recognizing these assets can help professionals identify existing strengths within the communities they serve, which they can support and build upon. Additionally, this perspective encourages working collaboratively with those impacted, acknowledging that they possess a deep reservoir of resources that foster resilience. *Shifting from a deficit-based approach to one that values these assets aligns* with antiracist practices and supports efforts to promote social and racial justice.

The **Racism + Resilience + Resistance Integrative Study of Childhood Ecosystem (R³ISE)** model (Iruka et al., 2022) is a framework that aims to center the effects of racism within an ecological perspective while incorporating Yosso's **community cultural wealth model**. This model underscores the significant role structural racism plays in shaping developmental outcomes and emphasizes the strengths and resilience that communities of color harness to counteract systemic challenges. By synthesizing current research, the R³ISE model provides a comprehensive lens for understanding how racism intersects with cultural resources to influence child development.

There are two prominent frameworks often used to understand the role of racism and other systems of oppression in the development of youth with marginalized identities. First, the **Integrative Model of Ethnic Minority Development** (also referred to as the Integrative Model) centers on the influence of an individual's social position (e.g., race, gender, class) and the societal stratification based on these positions on the development of children of color (Garcia Coll et al., 1996). A key component of the Integrative Model is how the environments that youth of color engage with either promote or inhibit the effects of racism and other oppressive systems. For instance, an individual school or neighborhood can mitigate or amplify the impacts of racism. **Neighborhood collective efficacy**, which refers to the social trust and cohesion within a community, has been associated with improved physical and mental health outcomes (Browning & Cagney, 2002; Xue et al., 2005). One study examining the relationship between race-related stress, perceived collective efficacy, and life satisfaction among Black adults found that life satisfaction was higher for those who reported greater levels of collective efficacy in the context of cultural race-related stress (Driscoll et al., 2015). Thus, greater levels of collective efficacy within a neighborhood is an example of a neighborhood characteristic that may inhibit the impacts racism for Black adults.

In addressing social stratification, the Integrative Model also considers the collective history of communities of color in resisting the impacts of racism. The adaptive culture within these communities offers strategies for responding to racism. For example, within Latine communities, cultural values often emphasize supporting children's educational achievement (Garcia Coll et al., 1996). The interplay between promotive or inhibiting environments and the adaptive cultural strategies of communities of color interacts with individual and family characteristics to predict developmental outcomes. The Integrative Model raises key questions about the roles that environments such as schools, healthcare systems, and neighborhoods can play in either reducing or exacerbating the impacts of racism, while also acknowledging the importance of cultural legacies in shaping responses to these challenges.

Second, the **Phenomenological Variant of Ecological Systems Theory (PVEST)** builds on ecological models by emphasizing the role of an individual's interpretation of their context and experiences in the developmental process (Spencer, 2006; Spencer et al., 2015). Unlike the bioecological and integrative models, PVEST centers on *how individuals make sense of their identities, experiences, and environments* to understand how racism may influence their development. PVEST goes beyond assessing whether environments are protective or inhibitive and instead considers how individuals *perceive* these contexts as supportive or limiting. For example, youth of color in the United States are more likely to live in racially and ethnically segregated neighborhoods with fewer resources (Menendian et al., 2021), which can result in fewer opportunities for mentoring relationships with adults (Owens, 2020). Mentoring relationships with adults are a significant potential asset in a youth's environment, associated with positive development (Bowers et al., 2021). While these conditions might be viewed as risk factors for youth of color and linked to structural racism, PVEST centers how youth of color perceive their environment, and thus what many may see as risk factor may not act as one for youth. To this end, researchers have found that **critical reflection** can act as a **protective factor** for positive youth development, even in the absence of high-quality mentors (Bowers et al., 2021). Specifically, youth of color who engage in critical thinking about social inequities recognize them as unjust, and understand their connection to structural issues report more positive development. This may occur because these youth are better able to contextualize the lack of support from mentors, thereby not perceiving this potential risk factor as inherently limiting (Suzuki et al., 2023).

The model posits that individuals adopt strategies in response to how they perceive stress in their environment. These strategies can either promote positive development or be maladaptive. Additionally, some strategies appear beneficial in the short term but lead to negative consequences over time. For example, a Latine undocumented college student who has traditionally not found support in educational settings may prioritize working to support paying for college, seen as promoting their well-being in the short term, while sacrificing time that could be used to access supportive campus resources, such as connecting to qualifying aid, which may have greater benefit for them in the long term (Hershberg et al., 2025). As individuals continue using these strategies, they become ingrained in their daily interactions and contribute to their evolving identities. Continuing the example, this student may struggle over time to balance education and work and may develop a negative identity of themselves as a student which may interfere with their academic performance over time (Hershberg et al., 2025). PVEST recognizes that these strategies and emerging identities are linked to developmental outcomes, which can vary depending on the developmental stage.

Overall, the PVEST model highlights the importance of **individual meaning-making** in shaping interactions with the environment (Spencer, 2006). In terms of understanding how racism influences development, this model underscores that *while racism can create vulnerabilities for people of color, the way individuals interpret and respond to their experiences can modify how they react and influence their contexts, leading to outcomes that are not predetermined to be negative* (Suzuki et al., 2023).

Choosing to be an antiracist professional requires commitment to personal reflection and growth, both key principles in human development. From our experience as authors in the field, we know that the frameworks discussed can provide valuable insights to guide your journey. You will be given opportunities to think about these frameworks in more concrete ways and put them into practice in Chapters 2–5.

Each of the aforementioned frameworks is useful in their own way and can help to promote thinking about antiracism and development in a particular way. The **bioecological model** encourages focusing on the person, process, context, and time. Reflecting on how racism appears in our current historical moment is an essential first step. This model reminds us that racism's manifestations can shift, so it is important to continually assess how it is reinforced in society and professional settings. The **Integrative Model** emphasizes the importance of specific contexts, like schools and healthcare systems, in either promoting or limiting the effects of racism. This means that antiracist work can involve developing or supporting elements in these environments that mitigate racism. However, **PVEST** reminds us not to assume that certain contexts will automatically lessen or amplify racism for youth of color; the individual's perception of these contexts is key (Spencer, 2006). Engaging directly with those affected and understanding how they experience racism is crucial.

The frameworks introduced here may seem abstract or complex, but we invite you to consider them as lenses, aligning with the title of this book, *Bringing Antiracism into Focus: Using Transformative Lenses to Reframe Professional Practice*. These frameworks are not meant to be a burden; rather, they are tools to help you understand and reveal the multiple, interacting parts of the social, physical, and internal worlds you work in. They provide a way to organize and make sense of complex dynamics and to help you think about your work with an antiracist perspective.

The goal is to equip you with a process to develop your critical developmental consciousness and become an antiracist professional who thoughtfully addresses and responds to challenges. **Critical consciousness**, a concept rooted in the work of Paulo Freire, Brazilian educator, philosopher, and author of *Pedagogy of the Oppressed*, involves understanding the historical, sociocultural, and political dynamics that shape environments and experiences (Freire, 1970). By fostering critical consciousness, individuals learn to "read the world" (Freire & Macedo, 1987) and identify how systemic oppression operates in their daily lives, enabling them to engage in actions that challenge and dismantle these structures (Suzuki et al., 2023). This book introduces **Early Career Steps for Developing an Antiracist Lens in Your Profession** and an **Antiracist Praxis Model** to help establish that identity.

Becoming an Antiracist Professional

Self-awareness and recognizing **personal biases** are crucial to this journey. Every individual holds biases shaped by their experiences, culture, and upbringing. Every individual carries biases shaped by their experiences, culture, and upbringing. The term "anti-bias" can be misleading if interpreted as a complete elimination of bias, which is unattainable. All humans have biases; they are inherent in the way our minds function. The reason you are alive and reading this book is because your mind engages in quick, automatic judgments and assumptions that help you navigate the world safely.

Consider this: when crossing the street and hearing the screech of tires, your brain makes split-second decisions based on past experiences (e.g., associating the sound with potential danger) and immediate assumptions (e.g., "I need to move quickly!"). While these protective responses are essential for survival, the same cognitive processes can lead to social biases and prejudices, which, if left unexamined, can have significant consequences.

When biases are observed and acknowledged, they are known as explicit (or conscious) biases. Biases that operate below conscious awareness are referred to as implicit (or unconscious) biases. Understanding both types is essential for professionals committed to creating equitable environments.

By recognizing and contextualizing these biases, professionals can better grasp how they influence behavior and decision-making. This self-awareness is foundational for meaningful change, particularly for those working in fields connected to individual development and socio-cultural interactions. Reflective practice helps professionals move toward a more equitable and intentional approach to their work. Ignoring bias does not make it disappear; much like ignoring race leads to colorblind racism, unexamined biases persist and shape actions in (sometimes) subtler, impactful ways.

To support ongoing personal reflection and development, we recommend strategies with our **Early Career Steps for Developing an Antiracist Lens in Your Profession** as well as our **Antiracist Praxis Model**, both described below, which encourage *continuous self-examination and learning*. Journaling, seeking feedback from peers and mentors, and engaging with diverse perspectives can help you identify areas for growth. Regular reflection helps align behavior with antiracist principles, an essential aspect of professional practice.

Engaging in difficult conversations is another significant part of this journey. Discussing race, bias, and systemic inequities can be uncomfortable but is necessary for both personal and professional growth. **Intellectual humility** is key, as is recognizing the nuanced interplay between opinions, lived experiences, and academic knowledge. The activities in this book encourage embracing vulnerability and openness during these dialogues. Notice your own defensive reactions and attempt to use these reactions as entry points for gaining deeper self-knowledge (Sensoy & DiAngelo, 2017). Understanding how your **social positionality** (e.g., race, class, gender, sexuality, ability) informs your perspectives enhances your capacity to create an environment where others feel encouraged to share their experiences and viewpoints (DiAngelo & Sensoy, 2019).

Integrating antiracist practices into daily professional tasks is vital for sustaining this commitment. This book will prompt you to explore ways to embed antiracist principles in your work through equitable decision-making, inclusive policies, and advocacy for marginalized groups. Even small, consistent actions can create significant change over time, reflecting the principles of ongoing growth in human development.

Building alliances and networks is crucial for supporting antiracist work. Connect with colleagues who share your commitment to equity and inclusion. Collaborate on initiatives, share resources, and support each other in addressing challenges. These networks provide a valuable support system and amplify the impact of your efforts, mirroring the importance of social support systems in human development (Abramovitz & Blitz, 2015).

Mentorship and continuous learning play a vital role in fostering an antiracist professional identity. Seek out mentors, allies, and co-conspirators who can guide you in your antiracist journey and provide feedback on your progress. Participate in ongoing education through workshops, seminars, and courses focused on diversity, equity, and inclusion. Staying informed about the latest developmental research and practices will help you remain committed in your antiracist work, aligning with the developmental psychology focus on lifelong learning and development.

Early Career Steps for Developing an Antiracist Lens in Your Profession

The **Early Career Steps for Developing an Antiracist Lens in Your Profession** provides a comprehensive approach for early-career professionals to integrate

Foundations: Antiracist Developmental Frameworks and Models

antiracist principles into their practice. These steps emphasizes the ongoing development of an antiracist perspective, encouraging continuous reflection and proactive learning throughout one's career. You will have opportunities to apply these steps in Chapters 2–5 through case studies, critical questions, and various profession-specific activities. By fostering an understanding of how to incorporate antiracist frameworks from the start, professionals are better equipped to navigate their roles with awareness, intentionality, and a commitment to equitable practices. These steps serves as a guide for building a foundation that evolves with one's growth and experiences in the field and helps develop the muscle memory needed to consider antiracist actions and perspectives in real time when in professional practice.

Box 1.2 Early Career Steps for Developing an Antiracist Lens in Your Profession

Build Your Awareness.
Examine how different ecological levels may contribute to impact.
Reflect on Personal Position and Bias.
Putting on an Antiracist Lens.
Engage with Various Stakeholders.
Identify Mentorship and Networks.
Participate in Professional Development and Continuous Learning.
Implement Antiracist Practices and Engage in Ongoing Reflection.
Ongoing Commitment to Antiracist Practice.

Build Your Awareness

Start by learning about some core concepts in antiracism. This includes ongoing learning about racism, systemic inequities based on race, and bias, antiracism, and intersectionality, among others. As you do this, be sure to both get a historical portrait of racism as well as understand the current state of these issues. Learn about these ideas generally and then also begin to understand racism within your future profession. Dive into the history and current state of these issues within your field. Ask about how racism has operated at both individual, institutional, and systemic levels in your field. As you enter your first professional setting, get to know the history of that community (or communities) in which you will work. What have their experiences of racism and resisting racism been? Learning this history will give you a sense of their readiness for antiracism and guide your future practice.

Examine Ecological Impacts

Think about the role of the different systems and how they impact racism in your profession. Consider the ways in which particular contexts across your profession may act as buffers to racism, or how you may introduce promoting factors in the environment. At the same time, consider the ways in which different settings may be inhibiting or further exacerbate the impacts of racism. As you begin to embed yourself in your professional setting, consider the communities you will work with. What are the assets in the families and communities you work in that may have a role to play?

Reflect on Personal Position and Bias

Take time to think about your own place within systems of power and privilege. Continuous self-awareness and reflection are vital for recognizing and addressing personal biases. This process involves regularly examining our beliefs, attitudes, and behaviors to identify how they might be influenced by stereotypes and prejudices. Reflect on biases you carry and how these could influence your professional behavior and decisions. Be honest with yourself and open to learning and changing. Build a habit of self-reflection, this is something you should cultivate and return to throughout your career.

Putting on an Antiracist Lens

Practice observing your environment through an anti-racist lens. This includes training yourself to identify subtle and overt forms of discrimination in professional settings. Ask yourself critical questions about who benefits from existing practices and who might be disadvantaged. Pay attention to policies, practices, and everyday interactions that perpetuate inequity. Learn how to articulate these observations clearly and thoughtfully.

Engage with Various Stakeholders

Actively seek out and reflect on diverse perspectives and experiences within your communities of interest. This includes not only other professionals in your field but includes the students, children, parents, clients, and communities you work with. This can include reading case studies, listening to personal narratives, or analyzing demographic data to understand how different people are impacted by the norms of your profession. Question who is being included or who is left out of particular spaces in your field and/or which perspectives are valued.

Identify Mentorship and Networks

Connect with mentors who embody anti-racist practices and can provide you with guidance and feedback. Mentors can provide valuable insights, feedback, and support as teachers navigate their antiracist journey. Effective mentorship involves honest conversations about race and equity, offering guidance on best practices, and encouraging continuous reflection and growth. This means you should build relationships on trust where you are prepared to be challenged and learn. Alongside mentorship, build a professional network that is focused on equity and antiracism. These networks offer opportunities for collaboration, sharing resources, and mutual support. Engaging with a community of like-minded professionals can provide the encouragement and accountability needed to sustain antiracist work. As you develop a community of other antiracist colleagues, be sure to celebrate each other in the small steps and successes! You can often find these communities through professional organizations in your field.

Participate in Professional Development and Continuous Learning

Continue your education in antiracism inside your future profession by engaging in professional development opportunities. Engaging in continuous learning allows you to stay up to date with new research and best practices in your field. Professional development can take many forms, including workshops, conferences, and online courses. Different forms of professional development each have unique benefits. Workshops can provide intensive, hands-on learning experiences. Conferences offer opportunities to hear from leading experts and network with other educators. Online courses can provide flexibility and access to a wide range of resources.

Implement Antiracist Practices and Engage in Ongoing Reflection

As you embark on your career, begin outlining how you can incorporate antiracist practices. Antiracist practices can happen at different levels and we recommend outlining those practices in your direct control at first. As you begin putting these into practice, reflect on how they go. Celebrate progress, even small successes, and consider how to adapt your approach when challenges arise. If things didn't go as planned or you are met with resistance, consider what you might do differently in the future. Ongoing reflection will help you continuously evaluate your effectiveness and improve your antiracist practice. It can be helpful to use theoretical frameworks or knowledge on racism introduced in this book or from your ongoing learning to reflect on your practice as they may help you develop a broader understanding.

Ongoing Commitment to Antiracist Practice

As you prepare for a career in antiracist practice, a commitment to this work cannot be overstated. Antiracist practice is a continual process that requires dedication to self-improvement and adaptation. It involves recognizing that there is always more to learn and unlearn, especially as societal contexts and understandings of race and equity evolve. By committing to this journey, you can better understand your role in either perpetuating or dismantling systemic inequities.

Putting it into Practice: Introducing the Antiracist Praxis Model

In addition to Early Career Steps for Developing an Antiracist Lens in Your Profession, there remains the question of "what to DO." As you enter the field, it's natural to feel an urge to take action, to translate the antiracist values you've cultivated into tangible changes. This drive to produce, to leave a mark, often reflects a broader cultural emphasis on external achievements and visible outcomes. We want to be change-makers. However, in antiracist work, genuine change relies on a balance between thoughtful action and the deep awareness that comes from critical reflection. Antiracist practice asks us to act in ways that simultaneously understand the realities of racism, view those realities as abnormal, view our own antiracism, and then act responsively to overtake racist power and policy in ways that are aligned with the realities and complexities of each situation (Kendi, 2019). That is a lot to balance when navigating a new profession!

We designed the Antiracist Praxis Model with this balance in mind. Moving beyond the simple impulse to "do something," this model offers a structured, step-by-step approach that guides you from awareness to action, helping you thoughtfully respond to issues of systemic, structural, and interpersonal racism in your professional environment. Whether addressing inequities in policies, practices, or day-to-day interactions, the Antiracist Praxis Model provides scaffolding for developmentally integrating antiracist values into your work in a way that is both impactful and reflective. Each step is intentionally sequenced to support your understanding of a situation before moving into action, emphasizing that in antiracist practice, context and thoughtfulness are key.

The Antiracist Praxis Model begins by helping you define the inequities present in a given situation, prompting you to gather necessary background information and consider the perspectives of those involved. Next, it encourages you to analyze the larger ecological factors that may be influencing the issue, such as institutional policies, community norms, or cultural biases, before determining the readiness of the community or organization for potential change. From there, the model supports you in brainstorming, preparing for, and implementing actions, always with an eye toward anticipating barriers and adapting your approach as you go. Ultimately, this model aims to cultivate a mindset of critical awareness, ensuring that actions you take have had a chance to be considered in an organized way, aligned with your core values, and grounded in a comprehensive understanding of the context.

The Antiracist Praxis Model is a tool to guide you in reflecting and putting into practice antiracism. It is meant to serve as a guide, a scaffold. You may very well find that your personal process is somewhat different from this in any given situation, particularly real-time scenarios, and that is absolutely fine! Know that it is still of value to practice with a model like the Antiracist Praxis Model to develop "muscle memory" of the broader categories of consideration that you will likely encounter. In general, the Praxis Model can be used when you are encountering a situation in your new career that you want to address. This can be used to determine how to react to everyday interactions within your workplace or policies and practices. This model emphasizes the importance of noticing and reflecting on instances of institutional and interpersonal racism, while also planning and taking actionable steps to address these issues in your professional environment. The detailed steps of the model will guide you through the process of integrating antiracist principles into your daily work, ensuring a balanced approach between understanding and action.

Box 1.3 Antiracist Praxis Model

Gaining an understanding of the situation
Develop a deeper understanding of the situation by defining the inequity(ies) at play, gathering perspectives, and assessing the role of different systems and community contexts.

Step 1: Identify inequity(ies)	Define the inequity(ies) at play. What is the background of the situation that is important to keep in mind? Who are the key figures?
Step 2: Perspective exploration	What are the perspectives of different people involved? What are the potential motivations of each group of people? What are the experiences they may come with to the situation? Outline how inequity impacts each of these people and their perspectives.
Step 3: Ecological analysis	Begin to breakdown the different processes and systems at play. How are these systems and processes shaped by racism?
Step 4: Identify community readiness	Gather information about how similar situations have been handled in the past? To do this, turn to your mentors and members of the community. What has already been tried? What were the reactions of different participants or within the community? How does this help you understand what change is possible in this situation? What does the community think are the next steps?

Brainstorming potential actions
Now that you've developed a deeper understanding, begin to imagine different actions to rectify the inequity(ies).

Step 5: Brainstorm potential actions	Identify what equity and antiracism may look like in this situation. Brainstorm short-term, action steps that you can take to achieve equity. Next brainstorm more long-term action steps you can take to achieve and maintain equity.

Step 6: Identify supportive resources	Identify two types of resources: (1) resources to help you better understand or implement change and (2) material resources that are needed to carry out the action steps you identified. (1) Identify those resources and support systems that can help you better understand the situation and implement action steps. This can include mentors, professional networks, and educational materials. (2) Additionally, identify what resources are needed to make change. These may be things like people, money, or materials that are needed to implement any of the action steps above.
Step 7: Reflect on potential barriers	It may be that some actions are not achievable as an early-career professional or for the community, given the community readiness, ecological factors, and perspectives you are taking into account. Look at each of your brainstormed action steps and outline barriers to implementation.

Putting it into action and reflecting

Having brainstormed potential actions as well as those resources and barriers that can support or limit those actions, develop an action plan that includes short-term and long-term steps. As part of an action-reflection cycle, make time to consider how taking action, or the actions of others, has changed your understanding of the inequity(ies) and how they can be undone to make changes to the next steps.

Step 8: Develop immediate and long-term personal action steps	Looking over your brainstorming, including the supportive resources and barriers for each step, identify those short- and long-term steps you can commit to. Outline what these are and what you need to do.
Step 9: Reflect and adapt	Reflect on your observations, noting your reactions, thoughts, and feelings. Analyze the dynamics of racism and your responses to these situations. Analyze and conceptualize your observations using theoretical frameworks and existing knowledge about racism and systemic inequities. Integrate insights gained from reflection into a broader understanding. Generate questions that arise from your reflections and conceptualizations. Identify areas for further exploration and make changes to your personal action plan as needed.

Applying the Antiracist Praxis Model in Your Professional Life

The Antiracist Praxis Model is a tool designed to help you actively integrate antiracist principles into your professional practice through a **scaffolded approach**. Think of it not as a rigid checklist that you must follow, but as a flexible framework that supports your *growth and development* as an antiracist practitioner. This model is a guide. It's natural for your personal process to vary across situations, especially in dynamic, real-time scenarios. This model offers a foundation for your responses, helping you develop *"muscle memory"* for accessing those key considerations and actions that foster antiracist practice in real-time professional contexts.

As you engage with the Antiracist Praxis Model, its purpose is to guide you in *reflecting and responding* thoughtfully to situations involving systemic, structural, or interpersonal racism. Each step encourages you to *pause, examine the context, and consider multiple perspectives*, ensuring that your actions are grounded in a deep understanding of the situation. The structure of this model can help you build skills in **critical reflection, situational analysis,** and **purposeful action** – all essential elements of developmentally informed antiracist practice.

Practicing the Antiracist Praxis Model in This Book

To help you internalize the Antiracist Praxis Model, this book provides the following scaffolded opportunities for **guided practice**:

- **Practical Examples**: Each chapter features developmental, profession-specific vignettes in which the authors will guide you through a scaffolded analysis of how to apply the steps of the Antiracist Praxis Model to contemporary issues relevant to early-career practitioners. These examples model how each component of the model can become embedded in your regular practice.
- **Case Studies for Deep Analysis and Discussion**: These in-depth scenarios invite you to critically engage with the broader context, analyze the factors at play, and explore possible responses either individually or in a group. The case studies provide a structured opportunity to apply the model's steps on your own, allowing you to refine your approach and practice responding to realistic challenges without direct guidance from the authors.
- **Reflective Exercises and Activities**: Throughout the book, you'll encounter exercises that prompt self-reflection and encourage you to experiment with different approaches. These activities are designed to help you integrate the Antiracist Praxis Model into your professional skill set, strengthening your capacity for thoughtful, context-sensitive responses over time.

In addition, we encourage you to *collaborate with peers and mentors* as you work with the Praxis Model whenever possible. *Engaging in discussions, sharing your observations, and gathering feedback* can deepen your understanding and reinforce your antiracist commitments. These collaborative experiences are invaluable in building a sustainable, developmentally informed antiracist practice that can evolve alongside your professional growth.

Developing a Sustainable Antiracist Practice

By regularly engaging with the Antiracist Praxis Model, you're constructing a *developmentally grounded, adaptable framework* for addressing inequity in your work. Each practice opportunity fosters habits of inquiry, intentionality, and action, which will serve you well throughout your career.

As you continue through this book, embrace this chance to develop as an antiracist practitioner who recognizes and meaningfully addresses issues of inequity. The Antiracist Praxis Model provides a structured yet flexible pathway that grows with you, helping you to respond thoughtfully, critically, and effectively. Over time, this approach will allow you to build a practice of antiracism that is enduring, proactive, and grounded in a deep understanding of developmental principles and professional context.

Chapter Summaries

Chapter 2: Examining and Resisting Racism through Psychology

This chapter introduces readers to the ongoing conversations regarding antiracism within psychology. Diving into ecocultural theory, ethnotheories, critical consciousness, empowerment, and resilience, readers will analyze central concepts in understanding and resisting racism. Readers will consider critical issues in the field, including the lack of representation for people of color within psychological research, measurement, and assessment. Antiracist strategies in the field will be introduced alongside professional resources for cultivating an antiracist identity within psychology. This chapter emphasizes connecting theory with application to foster a critical understanding of racism that can both support the well-being of individuals and foster systems change.

Chapter 3: Antiracist Developmental Teaching in PK-12 Education

Chapter 3 addresses systemic issues in PK-12 education, such as disparities in discipline and curriculum, and emphasizes the importance of developing critical consciousness and racial literacy. By expanding Vygotsky's Zone of Proximal Development to include race and a critical look at culture, the chapter redefines its application. Through case studies, practical examples, and guided activities, readers will reflect on teacher positionality, the way teacher identities mediate experiences for students, notice educational bias, and integrate antiracist practices with developmental theory to confront and challenge educational inequities.

Chapter 4: An Antiracist Developmental View of Higher Education

Chapter 4 guides readers in integrating antiracist principles into their higher education practice within child and adolescent development fields. Using the Multicontextual Model for Diverse Learning Environments (MMDLE) as an extension of Bronfenbrenner's bioecological systems model, the chapter examines how systemic racism, implicit bias, and power structures affect student development, especially for racially minoritized groups. Emphasizing intersectionality, critical consciousness, and mentorship, readers will explore ways to affirm student identity and foster inclusive educational spaces. Through practical examples, reflective exercises, and guided applications, this chapter encourages recognizing institutional inequities and engaging in reflective practice, proactive advocacy, and equitable policy development.

Chapter 5: Antiracist Approaches for Allied Health Professionals

In this chapter, readers will learn to examine the health of individuals and communities through an antiracist lens. Readers will apply bioecological systems theory and new understandings of the physiological effects of racism to analyze how institutionalized, personally mediated, and internalized racism affects physical and mental health. The chapter offers those entering allied health fields a variety of antiracist strategies, which, when taken up collaboratively with affected communities, can improve the health and well-being of children, adolescents, and families. Readers will explore the social determinants of health and racism-related stress and trauma by critiquing case studies and conducting key informant interviews. Key concepts, examples, and activities will prompt readers to employ an antiracist lens as they integrate theory, reflection, and action into a Praxis Model fundamental to changing social and environmental health conditions and disrupting racism at interpersonal and systems levels.

Critical Questions

1 Name three ways you can **model antiracist practices** in your field, and how this may improve outcomes for the people you serve.

2 Describe how **systemic racism** influences **professional practices** in your field, and why addressing it matters.
3 Identify one way **racism** impacts a **child's development** and explain how professionals can address this.
4 Provide an example of how professionals can use frameworks like the **bioecological model** to address systemic inequities.
5 Explain how understanding **intersectionality** can help professionals create more equitable practices.

References

Abramovitz, M., & Blitz, L. V. (2015). Moving toward racial equity: The undoing racism workshop and organizational change. *Race and Social Problems, 7*(2), 97–110.

Alhusen, J. L., Bower, K. M., Epstein, E., & Sharps, P. (2016). Racial discrimination and adverse birth outcomes: An integrative review. *Journal of Midwifery & Women's Health, 61*(6), 707–720.

Bonilla-Silva, E. (2015). The structure of racism in color-blind, "post-racial" America. *American Behavioral Scientist, 59*(11), 1358–1376.

Bonilla-Silva, E. (2017). What we were, what we are, and what we should be: The racial problem of American sociology. *Social Problems, 64*(2), 179–187.

Bowers, E. P., Bolding, C. W., Rapa, L. J., & Sandoval, A. M. (2021). Predicting contribution in high achieving Black and Latinx youth: The role of critical reflection, hope, and mentoring. *Frontiers in Psychology, 12*, 681574.

Bronfenbrenner, U., & Morris, P. (2006). The bioecological model of human development. In R. M. Lerner & W. Damon (Eds.), *Handbook of child psychology: Vol. 1. Theoretical models of human development* (6th ed., pp. 793–828). Wiley.

Browning, C. R., & Cagney, K. A. (2002). Neighborhood structural disadvantage, collective efficacy, and self-rated physical health in an urban setting. *Journal of Health and Social Behavior, 43*(4), 383–399.

Cauce, A. M., Coronado, N., & Watson, J. (1998). *Conceptual, methodological, and statistical issues in culturally competent research*. In M. Hernandez & M. R. Isaacs (Eds.), *Promoting cultural competence in children's mental health services* (pp. 305–329). Paul H. Brookes Publishing Co.

Coll, C. G., Crnic, K., Lamberty, G., Wasik, B. H., Jenkins, R., Garcia, H. V., & McAdoo, H. P. (1996). An integrative model for the study of developmental competencies in minority children. *Child Development, 67*(5), 1891–1914.

Collier, A. R. Y., & Molina, R. L. (2019). Maternal mortality in the United States: Updates on trends, causes, and solutions. *Neoreviews, 20*(10), e561–e574.

Collins, P. H. (2019). The difference that power makes: Intersectionality and participatory democracy. In O. Hankivsky, & J. S. Jordan-Zachery (Eds.), *The Palgrave handbook of intersectionality in public policy* (pp. 167–192). Palgrave Macmillan.

Combahee River Collective. (1977/1983). A Black feminist statement. In C. Moraga & G. Anzaldua (Eds.), *This bridge called my back: Writings by radical women of color* (2nd ed., pp. 210–218). Kitchen Table: Women of Color Press (Original work published 1977).

Crenshaw, K. (1991). Mapping the margins: Intersectionality, identity politics, and violence against women of color. *Stanford Law Review, 43*(6), 1241–1299. https://doi.org/10.2307/1229039.

Delgado, R., & Stefancic, J. (2017). Chapter II. Hallmark critical race theory themes. In *Critical Race Theory* (3rd ed., pp. 19–43). New York University Press.

DiAngelo, R., & Sensoy, Ö. (2019). "Yeah, but i'm shy!": Classroom participation as a social justice issue. *Multicultural Learning and Teaching, 14*(1), 20180002.

Driscoll, M. W., Reynolds, J. R., & Todman, L. C. (2015). Dimensions of race-related stress and African American life satisfaction: A test of the protective role of collective efficacy. *Journal of Black Psychology, 41*(5), 462–486.

Freire, P. (1970). *Pedagogy of the oppressed.* Seabury Press.

Freire, P., & Macedo, D. P. (1987). *Literacy: Reading the word and the world.* Bergin & Garvey Publishers.

Gaylord-Harden, N., Adams-Bass, V., Bogan, E., Francis, L. A., Scott, J., Seaton, E., & Williams, J. (2020). *Addressing inequities in education: Considerations for Black children and youth in the era of COVID-19.* Society for Research in Child Development.

Gee, G. C., Walsemann, K. M., & Brondolo, E. (2012). A life course perspective on how racism may be related to health inequities. *American Journal of Public Health, 102*(5), 967–974.

Gjerde, P. F. (2004). Culture, power, and experience: Toward a person-centered cultural psychology. *Human Development, 47*(3), 138–157.

Gorski, P. (2016). Rethinking the role of "culture" in educational equity: From cultural competence to equity literacy. *Multicultural Perspectives, 18*(4), 221–226.

Helms, J. E., Jernigan, M., & Mascher, J. (2005). The meaning of race in psychology and how to change it: A methodological perspective. *American Psychologist, 60*(1), 27.

Hershberg, R. M., Veritch Woodside, V. D., Durán, S., Rodriguez, J. L., & Gonzalez, A. B. (2025). Applying PVEST to identify the diverse coping and identity resources with which DACAmented and undocumented Latine students navigate their journeys to and through higher education. *American Journal of Community Psychology,* 1–14.

Hochschild, J. L. (1996). *Facing up to the American dream: Race, class, and the soul of a nation.* Princeton University Press.

Hughes, D., Rodriguez, J., Smith, E. P., Johnson, D. J., Stevenson, H. C., & Spicer, P. (2006). Parents' ethnic-racial socialization practices: A review of research and directions for future study. *Developmental Psychology, 42*(5), 747.

Iruka, I. U., Gardner-Neblett, N., Telfer, N. A., Ibekwe-Okafor, N., Curenton, S. M., Sims, J., ... & Neblett, E. W. (2022). Effects of racism on child development: Advancing antiracist developmental science. *Annual Review of Developmental Psychology, 4*(1), 109–132.

Jones, C. P. (2000). Levels of racism: A theoretical framework and a gardener's tale. American Journal of Public Health, 90(8). 1212–1215.

Kendi, I. X. (2019). *How to be an antiracist.* One World, A Trademark of Penguin Random House, LLC.

Leonardo, Z., & Manning, L. (2017). White historical activity theory: Toward a critical understanding of white zones of proximal development. *Race Ethnicity and Education, 20*(1), 15–29.

Lindsay, C. A., & Hart, C. M. D. (2017). Teacher race and school discipline. *Education Next, 17*(1), 72–78.

Menendian, S., Gailes, A., & Gambhir, S. (2021). *The roots of structural racism: Twenty first century racial residential segregation in the United States.* Othering and Belonging Institute. https://belonging.berkeley.edu/roots-structural-racism

Owens, A. (2020). Unequal opportunity: School and neighborhood segregation in the USA. *Race and Social Problems, 12*(1), 29–41.

Parenteau, A. M., Boyer, C. J., Campos, L. J., Carranza, A. F., Deer, L. K., Hartman, D. T.,& Hostinar, C. E. (2023). A review of mental health disparities during COVID-19: Evidence, mechanisms, and policy recommendations for promoting societal resilience. *Development and Psychopathology, 35*(4), 1821–1842.

People's Institute for Survival and Beyond. (2025). Undoing racism community organizing workshop.

Saleem, F. T., Anderson, R. E., & Williams, M. (2020). Addressing the "myth" of racial trauma: Developmental and ecological considerations for youth of color. *Clinical Child and Family Psychology Review, 23*(1), 1–14.

Seaton, E. K. (2020). A luta continual: Next steps for racism research among Black American youth. *Child Development Perspectives, 14*(4), 244–250.

Sensoy, O., & DiAngelo, R. (2017). *Is everyone really equal? An introduction to key concepts in social justice education.* Teachers College Press.

Smedley, A., & Smedley, B. D. (2005). Race as biology is fiction, racism as a social problem is real: Anthropological and historical perspectives on the social construction of race. *American Psychologist, 60*(1), 16.

Spencer, M. B. (2006). Phenomenology and ecological systems theory: Development of diverse groups. In R. M. Lerner (Ed.), *Handbook of child psychology: Theoretical models of human development* (6th ed., Vol. 1, pp. 829–893). John Wiley & Sons, Inc.

Spencer, M., Harpalani, V., Cassidy, E., Jacobs, C. Y., Donde, S., Goss, T. N., ... & Wilson, S. (2015). Understanding vulnerability and resilience from a normative developmental perspective: Implications for racially and ethnically diverse youth. In D. Cicchetti, & D. J. Cohen (Eds.), *Developmental psychopathology: Volume one: Theory and method* (pp. 627–672). John Wiley & Sons, Inc.

Suzuki, S., Johnson, S. K., & Ferreira van Leer, K. (2023). Situating critical consciousness within the developmental system: Insights from the Phenomenological variant of ecological systems theory. In L. J. Rapa & E. B. Godfrey (Eds.), *Critical consciousness: Expanding theory and measurement* (pp. 41–62). Cambridge University Press. https://doi.org/10.1017/9781009153751

Syed, M. (2016). Power and agency in conceptualizing life stages as master narratives. *Human Development, 59*, 317–323. https://dx. doi.org/10.1159/000455016

Syed, M., Santos, C., Yoo, H. C., & Juang, L. P. (2018). Invisibility of racial/ethnic minorities in developmental science: Implications for research and institutional practices. *American Psychologist, 73*(6), 812.

Tai, D. B. G., Shah, A., Doubeni, C. A., Sia, I. G., & Wieland, M. L. (2021). The disproportionate impact of COVID-19 on racial and ethnic minorities in the United States. *Clinical Infectious Diseases, 72*(4), 703–706.

Trent, M., Dooley, D. G., & Dougé, J. (2019). The impact of racism on child and adolescent health. *Pediatrics, 144*(2), e20191765. https://doi.org/10.1542/peds.2019-1765

US Department of Education Office for Civil Rights. (2014). Civil rights data collection data snapshot: School discipline. Issue brief no. 1.

Wang, M. T., Henry, D. A., Smith, L. V., Huguley, J. P., & Guo, J. (2020). Parental ethnic-racial socialization practices and children of color's psychosocial and behavioral adjustment: A systematic review and meta-analysis. *American Psychologist, 75*(1), 1.

Xue, Y., Leventhal, T., Brooks-Gunn, J., & Earls, F. J. (2005). Neighborhood residence and mental health problems of 5-to 11-year-olds. *Archives of General Psychiatry, 65*(5), 554–563.

Yosso, T. J. (2005). Whose culture has capital? A critical race theory discussion of community cultural wealth. Race Ethnicity and Education, 8(1), 69–91.

Chapter 2

Examining and Resisting Racism through Psychology

Introduction

Context and Relevance

The field of psychology has begun to recognize and address its role in racism in the United States. In 2021, the American Psychological Association (APA) issued an official apology for its role in maintaining and contributing to racism (APA, 2021). Other scholarly societies which represent subdisciplines of psychology have followed suit. For example, the Society for the Research on Child Development has developed an antiracism task force to outline antiracism principles and accountability measures for this organization of developmental psychologists. These statements offer a starting place to begin to navigate antiracism within psychology.

These recent examinations have identified the multiple ways in which psychology has perpetuated racism (Awad et al., 2024). These begin through the teaching of psychology within the university, which often does not include the perspectives of people of color, an introduction to antiracist praxis, or the limitations of psychological assessments (APA Division 45 Warrior's Path Presidential Task Force, 2020). Additionally, areas of psychology that require accreditation, such as counseling and clinical psychology, do not incorporate adequate protections for prejudice and discrimination nor do they incorporate concepts such as critical consciousness. This chapter will introduce such concepts and is a starting point to exploring these issues more deeply.

We can explore psychology's role in creating inequities by race and perpetuating racism across multiple avenues. Psychology provides the backbone for many assessments used in education, health settings, and social services. Many of these assessments have not been validated within communities of color and often are used in ways that may perpetuate racial inequities. For example, researchers have found that communities of color, including Black, Latine, Asian American, and Indigenous American youth, have higher rates of depression than white youth (McLaughlin et al., 2007; Rodriquez et al., 2018). There is evidence that different racial and ethnic groups internalize and/or express symptoms differently which means it may not be appropriate to use the same assessments across racial and ethnic groups (Anderson & Mayes, 2010). In another example, the use of baseline standardized test scores in psychology doctoral programs disproportionately impacted student of color applicants, even though applicants, regardless of standardized test scores, showed competence in coursework grades (Gómez et al., 2021). These are two examples of how many assessments, developed in part by psychologists, have been used to maintain racism. Over time psychology has developed and supported the use of measurements on intelligence (e.g., IQ) and ability which have been used to support ideologies that support a racial hierarchy, such as contributing to knowledge supporting the eugenics movement in the early 1900s or the boarding school systems for Native Americans (Cummings Center, 2021; Guthrie, 1976). Lastly, racial and ethnic disparities can be seen in the workforce where APA found that 83% of psychologists identified as White, while accounting for 60% of the U.S. adult population in 2019 (APA, 2020). Together, this paints a picture of different ways the field of psychology creates and maintains racism.

This chapter will introduce key theories from psychology which can guide us in antiracist practice. You will then be introduced to some key issues in the field of psychology that contribute to racism. Next, the chapters discusses key subfields and practical resources to consider the ways psychologists and the field of psychology can begin to redress the harm caused by racism. The chapter ends with some reflection and practice activities to apply concepts introduced.

This chapter's key features include:

- Theories to Examine and Resist Racism in Psychology
- Critical Issues and Practices related to Racism within Psychology
- Developing an Antiracist Professional Identity within Psychology
- Reflection and Practice Activities
- Recommended Resources

Theories to Examine and Resist Racism in Psychology

Chapter 1 introduced a number of core theories to help us understand the role of racism in the development of children and adolescents. These theories include the bioecological model, the Phenomenological Variant of Ecological Systems Theory (PVEST), the Integrative Model of Ethnic Minority Development, and the Racism + Resilience + Resistance Integrative Study of Childhood Ecosystem (R³ISE) model. These theories were developed within psychology or closely allied fields and are useful tools in examining the role of racism in human development and psychology. For those of you considering careers in psychology – whether that is as a future clinician, marriage family therapist, or researcher – we urge you to familiarize yourself with these theories as a starting place. This chapter will complement those theories by introducing additional psychological theories and concepts that are central to understanding and resisting racism.

Ecocultural Theory and Ethnotheories

Culture influences the everyday activities that children participate in. This includes activities within the family, school, and neighborhood – within and across microsystems. In this way, culture shapes the everyday activities of children and adolescents, shaping their development (Fuller & García Coll, 2010; Weisner, 2002). **Ecocultural theory**, which highlights the role of cultural values in driving individuals, beliefs, perceptions, and behaviors, is a traditional framework within the field (Weisner, 2002). These cultural values shape the daily routines of families alongside other ecological demands such as economic pressures, larger social norms, and resources in the community. Ecocultural theory asks us to consider the ways in which specific cultural and ecological circumstances families find themselves in shape their behaviors and subsequent child development.

There are multiple ways in which we might understand how culture shapes different developmental processes. One such way has been a focus on the role of **ethnotheories** within the family microsystem. Ethnotheories are those cultural beliefs that parents have about their parenting and children's development. These beliefs, in turn, shape parents' behaviors with their children (Harkness et al., 2010). These beliefs are often taken for granted by parents, such as ideas about sleep schedules or appropriate expected behavior, which families do not question but are shaped by culture. In an ethnographic study with 88 families in the United States, Annette Lareau (2011) famously documented differences in how affluent and low-income parents in the United States differed in their beliefs about children's development and thus how they structured their children's time. Specifically, she found that more affluent families in the United States were interested in cultivating their children's cognitive and intellectual abilities and thus structured their time to include more explicit learning activities, such as talking and reading activities or enrolling children in extra-curricular activities. In contrast, parents with low incomes tended to reflect a more natural growth attitude toward children, responding to everyday emotional and material needs as they came up for their children and giving their children more control over their free time. This example points to how parents' beliefs about childhood, parenting, and child rearing shape how they respond to children and organize their activities and time. They also include more explicit beliefs that parents express regarding parenting. For example, parents may state outright their ideas about the importance of having a routine for infants and toddlers.

Beyond microsystems, cultural beliefs can also guide how we understand how families interact with other microsystems. Scholars have examined how parents' beliefs about what qualities were related to success in schools looked differently across culture. In a survey of parents across 7 countries (Italy, Spain, Poland, Sweden, the Netherlands, the United States, and Australia) researchers found that within the United States, parents more narrowly focused on cognitive competence, such as the ability to concentrate well and paying attention as compared to emotional or social competence, such as being concerned with others and being polite, which was rated more highly by parents in other countries (Feng et al., 2020). Additionally, the researchers found higher agreement in those beliefs among those parents from countries that were "culturally closer" (e.g., Italy and Spain; United States, and Australia). This research points to the ways in which culture guides the ways in which families conceptualize development as it relates to other microsystems. Moreover, these cultural beliefs can also guide how they interact with these microsystems. In research with low-income Latine families attending public preschool programs, McWayne and colleagues (2019) have pointed out that cultural values help us understand when, how, and why parents engage in their children's school. Cultural beliefs about children and their development thus shape the everyday activities and interactions that children are exposed to.

If we use an antiracist lens, we can further see how ecocultural theory and ethnotheories can help us understand systemic disparities by race and ethnicity. Particularly, these concepts offer tools in which to examine how the cultural values of different ethnic and racial groups may differ from the microsystems that children from these groups are embedded in. The lack of cultural congruence between home and school environments, for example, may result in differential outcomes. In these ways, *discontinuities between cultural expectations and behavioral scripts may help us understand how racism manifests structurally, is reified in institutions of education, and contributes to educational inequities.* Additionally, it points to the importance of **cultural humility** (see more in Chapter 5) and considering the role of culture in shaping access to and informing work with different communities.

Empowerment and Resilience

Empowerment is a popular psychological concept. Given its widespread use from social movements to self-help texts, empowerment is often understood in multiple ways by different people. Within psychology, it is understood as attaining power and control over one's circumstances (Lord & Hutchison, 1993; Rappaport, 1981). Using an ecological framework, we can broaden this definition. We can understand empowerment as something possible across multiple systems – the individual, specific microsystems such as family or neighbors, or exosystems like larger communities one is embedded in. Empowerment can be both applied to individuals or groups. In this way, individuals or groups of people can go through a process of gaining greater control over their lives and attain meaningful goals they set for themselves (Maton, 2008). The aim of empowerment is centered around those goals that individuals or communities set for themselves. This could be having greater control over resources for schools in one's neighborhood, or an individual having the resources to leave a violent relationship. Even at the individual level, empowerment is something achieved socially.

Resilience is the process of adaptation and change in an individual faced with hardship, trauma, and stress to support their own well-being (Rutter, 1993). Psychologists have long been interested in how individuals develop and demonstrate resilience in the face of obstacles in their life. The concept can help us understand how two individuals facing similar adversities may have different outcomes. How individuals draw on their resources or internal capabilities to achieve well-being positions us to look to the strengths that individuals have. These strengths can be supported or cultivated to help individuals navigate such hardships. Typically, the obstacles that individuals face are a result of structural differences in oppression.

Resilience has been theorized to include awareness, intention, action, reflection, and maintenance (Brodsky et al., 2011). Individuals must become aware of the power dynamics and structures that have led to the stress they are facing and understand that they can be changed. For example, Latine youth who are facing difficulties in school and doing badly in their academics might first come to an awareness that their difficulties may be related to the differences in support that they are receiving or that their school is under resourced, or that teachers have low expectations for them given their ethnicity. Next, intention is the internal ability to identify actions to change their circumstances. Continuing the example, the Latine youth might identify a goal to improve their academic performance and identify specific resources in their community – afterschool programs or mentoring adults – or working with other Latine students in similar situations to improve their grades. The individual then carries this out in action, by working toward their goal. As they take these actions, they engage in reflection to assess whether they are successful in meeting their goals. Continuing the example, the Latine youth may reflect on the ways their strategies have resulted (or not) in better grades and identify new strategies to achieve their goals or adjust their goals. Lastly, resilience includes maintaining their well-being and ensuring their approaches allow them to continue their own positive development.

Given the complementary nature of empowerment and resilience to support individuals in overcoming structural oppression, Brodsky & Cattaneo (2013) have proposed a conceptual model to link them. The resulting **Transconceptual Model of Empowerment and Resilience** (TMER) brings together these concepts to describe a process where individuals can overcome adversity through personal growth and action (resilience) as well as work to create larger social change regarding the larger social issue (empowerment). In the example provided, this means that a Latine student may undertake personal actions to improve their academics as well as work with other Latine students to transform the underlying conditions that create disparities in academic scores for Latine students more broadly

Psychologists can utilize TMER as framework to not only support individual changes but also address structural inequities. Stated differently, a focus on resilience and individual change alone may result in increased well-being for the target individual but does not change those conditions that have led to the issue in the first place. From an antiracist lens, TMER promotes supporting individuals to understand and identify actions to overcome the impacts of racism in their own life, while partnering with others to change those same structures that reinforce racism. *The twin goals of resilience and empowerment acknowledge that we must attend to individual needs and well-being in transformational work.*

Critical Consciousness

A dynamic process, **critical consciousness** describes how individuals develop an awareness of systems of oppression and engage in actions to undo it (Diemer et al., 2016; Freire, 1970). Critical consciousness originally comes from Paulo Freire, a Brazilian educator who through literacy work with laborers developed *conscientização* (conscientization in English). Through learning to read the world, Freire felt that individuals could gain a new understanding of their reality and work to transform it. Particularly interested in the class struggles of Brazil, his literacy circles provided people an opportunity to examine the historical, political, and sociocultural context in which they found themselves. In this way, individuals would begin to understand oppression in their own lives. As individuals better understood those conditions, they were encouraged to take actions to transform them to better support their well-being. As they undertook actions to transform that oppression they would often better understand that oppression. Witnessing this, Freire identified the importance of the cycle of action and reflection, or **praxis**, in understanding and transforming oppression.

While critical consciousness emerged within education, it has increasingly been utilized within psychology (Diemer et al., 2016). Similar concepts, such as **sociopolitical development** which describes the process in which individuals understand, analyze, and gain the socioemotional and psychological capacity to understand and resist oppression, have also emerged within psychology (Watts et al., 2003). Psychologists have broken down critical consciousness into three core components – critical reflection, motivation/efficacy, and critical action. Critical reflection is the growing understanding of inequities, systems of oppression and injustice. This may be along one axis of injustice (e.g., racism) or multiple (e.g., racism and sexism) and can change over time. There are multiple terms used to capture this second construct such as motivation, political efficacy, and political agency, all aiming to capture an individual's beliefs in their ability to address the injustices. Lastly, critical action refers to those actions that individuals engage in to transform injustice. These actions may be individual or collective. Together psychologists and others have been interested in how critical consciousness can be fostered to transform systems of oppression, such as racism, and to better understand how critical consciousness is related to youth well-being, especially for youth of color.

Increasingly scholars recognize how critical consciousness increases the well-being of youth of color and may provide a link between student experiences and outcomes (Bowers et al., 2020; Seider et al., 2020). In these ways, critical consciousness may not only be important toward fostering communal change but also as a protective factor in experiencing oppression, such as racism.

Critical consciousness is a central concept for psychologists interested in understanding those processes related to resisting racism. The emerging literature on critical consciousness encourages us not only to better understand the conditions that foster it but also seek to cultivate it in communities of color as a protective mechanism for those individuals. Specific practices outlined below, such as healing justice and problematization, offer insights into how critical consciousness can be developed.

Taken together, these frameworks provide a foundation to begin engaging in antiracism within your future career as a psychologist. Ecocultural theory prompts us to consider the role of culture, and the ways that cultural beliefs and scripts may not be supported across contexts. Ethnotheories attunes us to the ways that culture drives parenting behaviors, shaping how children from different cultural backgrounds develop. The Transconceptual Model of Empowerment and Resilience encourages us to support individuals facing oppression by simultaneously encouraging individual actions to gain agency over their own circumstances while working with others to transform the conditions that result in their oppression. Lastly, critical consciousness gives us an understanding of how individuals can begin to understand racism, and other systems of oppression, and take action to undo it. With this foundation the chapter turns to critical issues in the field which create and sustain racism as well as practices antiracist psychologists can consider.

Critical Issues and Practices

Who Is Left Out of Psychological Research?

Understanding how the field of psychology has maintained racial inequities can be seen in how the field's knowledge base has been developed. Much of the empirical research within psychology has overutilized samples that do not reflect the world population (Syed et al., 2018). Joseph Henrich and colleagues (2010) examined top journals in psychology from 2003 to 2007 and found that over two-thirds of the samples came from the United States and 96% came from North America, Europe, Australia, and Israel. They labeled this population as WEIRD – coming from Western, Educated, Industrialized, Rich, and Democratic societies – and a problematic reality of psychology and allied fields. The reliance on this population as the majority of those who psychological research is conducted on is concerning as the majority of researchers use these samples to generalize to all people. In other words, psychological research is often applied to people beyond North America, Europe, Australia and Israel. The tendency within psychological research is to seek to understand universal processes, and, as such, researchers make claims regarding how research reveals truths about human development at large. Typically, these claims go unquestioned, leading readers and researchers alike to assume they have learned something universal that applies to all individuals.

While much of the research has focused on WEIRD populations, this does not mean it is representative of the different social identities within these populations. For example, research in the United States is largely based on samples of college students who are disproportionately White and middle or upper class. These samples often leave out Black, Latine, Asian, and Indigenous communities (Syed et al., 2018). Beyond race and ethnicity, sexual and gender minorities, foreign-born, neurodiverse, and people with differing physical abilities are often not included.

In addition to being excluded from the majority of research samples, *the perspectives, concerns, and experiences common to communities of color are also left out of research.* This means that our fields are missing key knowledge produced from these communities which can provide important information to understand psychology and development. For example, the National Institutes of Health and the National Science Foundation, which provide billions of dollars in funding for research in the United States, more often awards research funding to lead researchers who are White than Black (Chen et al., 2022; Ginther et al., 2011). Research has also found that Black researchers typically propose research topics more aligned with the concerns of their communities, such as research on racial health disparities or community-based prevention and that these topics are funded at lower rates (Hoppe et al., 2019). In other words, the topics that are of concern to Black researchers are less likely to be valued.

The inequalities in who is represented in research and whose knowledge is valued create ripple effects across the field and perpetuate inequities in society. As empirical research is increasingly used to support interventions like after-school programs or therapies, the lack of scrutiny to whether the research applies to diverse populations means that research can inadvertently be used to perpetuate racial inequities. *To combat this, you must critically consume research and question assumptions about what is known within the field.*

People of Color Are Often Left Out of Psychological Measures and Assessments

Psychological researchers and practitioners must contend with the ways the measures and assessments they use can perpetuate racism. Psychologists, across a variety of settings, use and develop measures and assessments. These assessments can be used to guide our understanding of specific phenomena – such as parental engagement in schools – or used as tools to diagnose and provide support to youth – such as internalizing disorders in youth (e.g., anxiety). Increasingly psychologists have begun to identify that these tools have been developed with limited connection to the lived experiences of people of color and their use may further disparities by race and ethnicity.

Continuing an example used earlier regarding the role of culture in shaping parent engagement, traditional measures of parent engagement in schools indicate that Latine parents are not engaged in their children's education (Steinberg et al., 1992). This is particularly distressing as there is a rich literature documenting the role of parental engagement on children's academic success (Castro et al., 2015; Fan & Chen, 2001). Traditional measures conceptualized school engagement primarily as those activities led by parents which promoted learning at home, such as reading or playing educational games, and promoted interaction with school, such as volunteering in school or communicating with teachers (Epstein, 2010). These views on parent engagement with schools disproportionately viewed that parents were responsible for initiating and sustaining engagement with schools. As scholars began outlining the ways in which Latine cultural values shaped Latine parent engagement with schools, questions emerged whether these traditional views on parent engagement with schools were accurate. Furthermore, research revealed many ways in which Latine parents were highly invested in and engaged in their children's education (McWayne et al., 2013; McWayne et al., 2016), countering the prevailing narrative that Latine parents were not engaged in their children's schools and raising questions regarding how parental involvement was being measured.

Scholars began outlining the ways that Latine parent cultural values shaped their engagement with schools. Building on this work, Christine McWayne and colleagues sought to measure these hypothesized relationships (McWayne et al., 2013). They developed a new measure of Parental Engagement of Families from Latine backgrounds (PELF). Using this measure, these scholars have documented the many ways that Latine parents engage in educational activities at home with their children. This work identified that Latine parents are engaged in many ways in their children's learning at home. Specifically, they found that there are three dimensions to home-based engagement with children's learning – teaching children the basics of social interactions and academics; providing children learning experiences beyond the basics; and efforts to instill a value of education as a tool for social mobility and future well-being (McWayne et al., 2016). This challenges previous conceptualizations of school engagement as solely one set of home-based practices and provides a more culturally grounded measure for parental engagement with Latine parents.

This example shows that regardless of your specific career within psychology you should carefully examine the measurements and assessments you use. You should consider how these measures were developed and how they included a diverse racial and ethnic set of participants. Additionally, you must recognize that these assessments may reinforce systemic beliefs of particular racial and ethnic groups as inferior or less than. As described above, by drawing on rich qualitative work with Latine families, McWayne and colleagues (2013) were able to develop more accurate measures to capture parental engagement with Latino families and support a shift in conceptualizing parental engagement with schools from a deficit lens to one that embraces families' assets (McWayne et al., 2019). Similar efforts to develop new measures and assessments that are valid with specific ethnic and racial groups are being taken across the field. Thus, as you examine those measures and assessments you may typically use also search for those being newly developed. These new measures and assessments may offer a more ecologically valid tool that you can adopt in your future practice.

Healing Justice

Critical practices in the field, such as healing justice, offer potential tools for antiracist psychological practice. In response to the devastation from Hurricane Katrina in New Orleans, Black feminists began to engage in a process to heal from oppression and take actions to improve their circumstances (Page, 2013). With an understanding that trauma results from systems of oppression, these women sought to both address the harm done as well as change the systems of oppression. This strategy of centering collective healing alongside taking action to change one's conditions has since been adopted by multiple communities. **Healing justice** seeks to build on the assets of communities, building on their existing knowledge and skills, to create spaces to come together to heal from oppression and take actions toward liberation (Ginwright, 2018). Through the development of collective spaces, healing justice aims to foster hope within communities impacted by racism or other systems of oppression. These spaces allow individuals to build a sense of community and belonging among those who have faced similar experiences. It seeks to develop routines that allow for connection, healing, and building hope. This framework explicitly acknowledges that the trauma and conditions that result from oppression are not something located within individual faults but rather are a result of the system.

Box 2.1 Implementing Healing Justice Practices: A Case Study on the Alaska Native Cultural Identity Project (CIP)

Addressing the marginalization that Indigenous students often report facing at universities, university staff, 5 Indigenous Elders, and 44 students engaged in an 8-week program entitled, "The Alaska Native Cultural Identity Project." The project was developed with explicit attention to healing justice as one of its primary topics and integrated healing justice approaches throughout its programs (Buckingham et al., 2023). To develop the program, the facilitators worked with Alaskan Native elders and drew from focus groups with undergraduate students and empirical literature to develop a structure for the 8-week program. Through this process, they identified the need for a program that integrated storytelling from Alaskan Native elders, activities that provided an opportunity for discussion and connection among Alaskan Native students, experiential learning activities, exploration of Alaskan Native cultural identity, and documentation of cultural strengths and identities. Student participants discussed how the space fostered a sense of community, building deep emotional connections between and among Alaskan Native elders and students. They discussed how these connections facilitated healing by meeting multiple needs of group members and creating opportunities for vulnerability and relationship building. Participants discussed wanting to develop other such spaces, suggesting empowerment and action. Buckingham and colleagues (2023) noted that the structure of the program was key to these outcomes and other psychologists should seek to partner with those communities they are working with to develop, facilitate, and evaluate their inventions toward healing and social change.

Problematization

Another tool in which psychologists can begin to support individuals' understanding of racism and other systems of oppression is problematization. Problematization is a technique in which you help others examine their own assumptions about reality and how it upholds power structures to develop a critical understanding of systems of oppression (Montero, 2009). Similar to the ways in which Freire utilized literacy circles to help laborers better understand the class dynamics in Brazil, problematization can be used in many situations. The process can be one of dialogue with others, utilizing photos (e.g., Lykes & Schieb, 2018), poetry (e.g., Cammarota & Romero, 2009), drawings (e.g., Krueger-Henney, 2014), or stories and testimonio (e.g., Fernández, 2024).

The process of problematization involves creating scenarios in which an individual is made to confront their own understanding of their experience, sowing doubt in their own understanding of how the situation may occur and creating an opportunity for a new understanding of that circumstance. Additionally, through developing a new understanding of their circumstances, they begin to imagine other possibilities for addressing the situation. This process should be grounded in everyday situations, allowing individuals to engage with concrete examples that are meaningful to them. Using these experiences as a starting point, problematization urges individuals to explore their historical conditions, examine them within their larger context, and discuss how they have been impacted. As they begin this reflection, individuals are confronted with the need to find new answers to understand their problem, developing a critical stance to their circumstances.

Martiza Montero (2009), a political psychologist, outlines specific conditions for the problematization process: listening, dialogue, taking care of the ways to participate in that dialogue, communication, humility and respect, and critique. She emphasizes the need for an empathetic and human process in which individuals are treated as equal agents in the dialogue. Additionally, she recognizes that the process is both a cognitive and emotional process. As individuals begin to develop new understandings of their circumstances, it may cause internal strife. The problematization process can happen between two or more people and through mutual exchange where all participants are meaningfully engaged. In this way, *problematization cannot be approached as a scholarly exercise in which one individual seeks to explain oppression to another, but rather an exchange of ideas over time that allows individuals to gain a new understanding of their circumstances.*

Partnering Directly with Impacted Communities

Collaborating directly with impacted communities provides psychologists and those communities more equitable approaches to addressing the impacts of racism. Community engagement is crucial to both developing programs and interventions as well as conducting evaluation and research in ways that support community goals.

Psychologists may often be called to use their expertise to address issues faced by or within communities of color. They may be asked to provide guidance on programs within the community that seek to address these issues. Alternatively, they may be asked to develop interventions, or programs, to make positive changes. It is important to remember that these issues may be a symptom of larger structural issues, such as racism. Traditional interventions utilize psychologists or other professionals as the experts around the issue. In this model, the psychologist has the answers and skills. Yet, as we have identified above, psychologists and psychological research have long ignored the experiences of communities of color and/or have promoted research in ways that have exacerbated inequities. Participatory approaches to interventions bring together those members of the community, including those most impacted, to identify, develop, and carry out programs to address the identified issue. For example, imagine a community is interested in addressing issues of homelessness in their neighborhood. Instead of taking programs off the shelf developed by psychologists and other professionals, a participatory intervention may bring together individuals experiencing homelessness and other neighbors to address the issue. This group would identify their goals for their work, gain a better understanding of the history and causes of homelessness in their communities, and develop action plans together.

Similar to interventions, researchers have identified community-engaged research, such as community-based participatory research or participatory action research, as centering the perspectives of impacted communities within research and allowing research to be grounded in their lived experiences (Wallerstein, 2021). Many psychological research traditions trace their roots back to Paulo Freire, Ignacio Martin-Baro, or other psychologists like Kurt Lewin. This research values working directly with community, incorporating local knowledge, and creating change within the lived realities of those they are partnering with (Minkler, 2004; Wallerstein & Duran, 2010). As such, a key component to community-engaged research is intentionally building the capacity of communities you are working with to engage in research (Lundy, 2006; McKay, 2010; Minkler, 2004). This is a shared goal, with those designing interventions and other community programs where building capacity of community members to identify goals, develop actions, and carry out programs is a part of the process. Both also require working with communities to build power for change. Such a change may be gaining funding for community-initiated programs or interventions and/or taking the results of research to transform policies or the local environment. See the discussion on *building community power* in chapter 5 for more information on what this can look like. Additionally, Gonzalez & Facilitating Power (2019) offer a useful introduction and guide to community engagement strategies.

Whether engaging in research, evaluation, program development, or interventions, *it is important to acknowledge the previous harm that psychologists, as practitioners and researchers, have done to communities.* This harm may include past and continuous misrepresentation, exploitation, and reinforcement of oppressive structures. Such harm may have been done by research conducted (Wallerstein & Duran, 2010) or by practitioners in these same communities. For these reasons, communities may mistrust psychologists and attempt to partner directly. Better understanding the histories of psychologists, academics and other professionals within those communities in which you aim to work can help you prepare to address such harm and build trust.

Building trust takes time. In a review of photovoice, a methodology used in community-engaged research, Hergenrather and colleagues (2009) found that among 31 projects, the average length of a time was over 7 months. This likely does not account for the time to build relationships and develop the project which occur before the projects began. McKay and colleagues (2010), working with war-affected young mothers in three different countries, highlight the significant investment of time that the projects took, including in building trust with and between young mothers and in their understanding of their control over the process. Thus, you should plan for and anticipate investing significant time in relationship building with those communities that you aim to work with.

In addition to such acknowledgments of past harm and investing time in building relationships, community-engaged research encourages reflectivity and critical reflection on the ways that power and privilege are a part of and circulate within the partnership (Chávez et al., 2003; Hagey, 1997; Nelson and Prilleltensky, 2005). As you begin a partnership, *you should reflect critically on the ways that power and privilege are a part of and circulate within the partnership.* Ongoing reflection on the circulation of power within the partnership can help you prevent the partnership from perpetuating those inequities in larger society. This reflection should continue throughout the partnership process.

Developing an Antiracist Professional Identity within Psychology

Antiracist Thinking across Psychology

There are multiple subdisciplines of psychology that offer important perspectives in addressing issues of racism and oppression within the field. Particularly we highlight here **Liberation Psychology**, **Community Psychology**, and **Critical Psychology**. While you may not chose to pursue degrees in these areas of psychology, you can find that these approaches are represented within multiple programs. For example, many counseling psychology programs also offer community psychology emphases. Alternatively, you can seek out resources from these subfields relevant to your discipline. As an example, if you are studying to become a developmental psychologist you might look for those working at the connection between critical psychology and developmental psychology. To this end, you might find scholars such as Erica Burman working in critical developmental psychology to be relevant. As you pursue your potential career in psychology, we encourage you to look to these subfields for inspiration and up-to-date information regarding antiracism within the field as well as specific skills that may support your development as an antiracist psychologist.

Critical Psychology

Perhaps best described as an approach to psychology, critical psychology challenges those assumptions and practices utilized within mainstream psychology and assert that they often are used to maintain injustice (Fox et al., 2009; Teo, 2015). Critical psychology rejects mainstream psychology's political neutrality and the stance that scientific work has objectivity. To this end, they see research in psychology often supporting social hierarchies and maintaining inequality. Additionally, these approaches critique psychology as too often focusing on the individual and ignoring the role of context and larger society as well as overemphasizing the role of individual values over community. Critical psychologists can be found in any subdiscipline – see for example, the work of Brendan Gough within social psychology, Erica Burman within developmental psychology, or Tod Sloan in counseling psychology or at the intersection of psychology with other disciplines, such as health psychology, see work by Kerry Chamberlain or psychology and law, see work by Dennis Fox. These theorists aim to peel back the assumptions within psychology and show that even despite individual psychologists' or the field of psychology's intentions to do no harm, the field maintains oppression.

Liberation Psychology

A subfield of psychology that emerged with the work of Ignacio Martín-Baró, **liberation psychology** is a movement to center the lived experiences of those experiencing oppression within psychology. Developed as a response to the civil war in El Salvador during the 1980s, Ignacio Martín-Baró pushed for a psychology "of – and by – the people," aiming to work alongside populations to hold a social mirror to themselves to better understand their circumstances and aim to improve it (Martín-Baró, 1996). For Ignacio Martín-Baró this was done by partnering with rural peasants to develop public opinion polls revealing their perspectives into the ongoing civil war and bringing their voices into the national conversation. These polls were a crucial tool to bring an oppressed group's perspective into the conversation but were also a tool to begin dismantling the common narratives about the gross inequities occurring. By partnering with those who were oppressed and developing research to better reflect their circumstances, the research sought to help them uncover the ways that larger systems oppress them. Partnering with oppressed communities directly, using research to better represent their realities, and supporting social change have been taken up by other psychologists.

Tenets of liberation psychology include recovering historical memory, de-ideologization of everyday experiences, virtues of the people, problematization, critical consciousness, and social change. We can use these tenets in antiracist work. First, liberation psychology reminds us to ensure we have a deep historical understanding. Liberation psychologists critique mainstream psychology for its ahistorical stance, arguing that a deep understanding of history is necessary to understand oppression. Thus, those psychologists interested in antiracism must gain an understanding of how racism has unfolded over time. This historical understanding will provide a clearer view into how racism manifests today. An example of how a historical perspective helps us understand contemporary racism is the work of Michelle Alexander (2012) and others who have helped chart how racism has existed in U.S. society over time as well as how it has remade itself to persist across different historical periods. Alexander (2012) has outlined how racism has been sustained in the United States by taking on different forms over time but continuing to maintain a system of racialized social control. Providing an overview of racism in the United States, she identifies three significant periods: (1) Slavery; (2) Jim Crow; (3) Mass Incarceration. She dissects these historical periods, illustrating how each has features that change to meet their historical circumstances to maintain a racial hierarchy within the United States. Gaining an understanding of racism and its history within the United States is a starting place.

Liberation psychology urges psychologists to work with those directly impacted by oppression, in this case racism, to uncover shared histories that may not be told in mainstream narratives. This work to uncover history directly with impacted communities also can foster critical consciousness through a process to better understand those conditions that have resulted in oppression. As you develop your professional identity – seek out opportunities to better understand the history of racism. At the same time, liberation psychologists also recognize that there are histories that may not be easily accessible, either because they have been rendered invisible by current structures or the histories have not been formally documented. Antiracist work may then require recovering collective historical memory related to the past and ongoing historical violence of slavery.

Box 2.2 Integrating Liberation and Counseling Psychology: A Case Study of Group Workshops Deconstructing Gender-Based Violence and Taking Action with Women of Burma

Working with refugee and internally displaced women in Burma in the 1990s, Norsworthy and Khuankaew (2004) sought to develop and implement a group intervention to address gender-based violence. This intervention sought to bring together components of Liberation Psychology and Counseling Psychology. The psychologists facilitated workshops on self-care, empowerment, oppression, and deconstructing violence against women. These workshops provided participants housing in a secure location and were conducted over four- to five-days, lasting 8 to 10 hours each day. Drawing on Liberation Psychology's use of problematization and goal for social change, the project intentionally worked with women to identify systems change in their communities. The groups also integrated self-reflection and normalization activities common to counseling psychology. To better problematize gender-based and structural violence against women, the psychologists utilized drawing activities of an island or mountain to guide women through identifying elements of violence. For example, using an island, the groups discussed how much of the island is below the surrounding waves, creating an unseen foundation for the island. Using this metaphor, they began to ask women to identify the unseen supports for gender-based violence. Continuing in this fashion, the women engaged in explicitly naming and deconstructing their ideas about gender-based violence. Together they identified how different institutional and policy structures supported violence as well as how violence was maintained through various cultural understandings. Throughout the workshop, the psychologists and participants engaged in deep listening. Having identified these supports, the women were led through identifying actions for social change. They were led through activities to identify transformative actions at the individual, family, community, organization, and institutional and societal levels. The workshops concluded with developing an action plan for women to carry out back in their local communities. In an evaluation of the workshops, participants discussed how they felt empowered by the process, more actively willing to contribute to address violence in their communities. At the same time, participants described the workshops as taxing as well as providing participants with hope. These workshops are an example of integrating counseling with centering taking action for social change within group settings.

Community Psychology

In response to the social movements of the 1960s as well as the community mental health movement, **community psychology** was developed in the United States. In contrast to medical models of one-on-one therapy, community psychologists sought to address social issues through **prevention programs** (in contrast to treatment) and to involve themselves in social change. Additionally, community psychologists aimed to move beyond the individual focus frequently found in psychology and emphasize that *individuals cannot be understood separately from their environments*. In other words, community psychologists take an ecological perspective to understanding social and psychological issues. James Kelly (1986) introduced an Ecological Theory which sought to understand human behavior in relationship to their environment. Similar to the Bioecological Model introduced in chapter 1, community psychologists consider the role of different levels of the environment on individuals. Nonetheless, Kelly's Ecological Theory differs from the Bioecological Model in its explicit attention to using research driven from the model in concert with local knowledge to create change with communities (Scarpa & Trickett, 2022). In this way, Ecological Theory is concerned with the role of using knowledge to shape community development and create change, whereas the Bioecological Model largely aims to contribute to growing scientific knowledge, and potentially, informing policy. Given these origins, community psychology has always been interested in addressing societal injustice, such as racism, and has sought to provide tools to address such injustices. Together, prevention, social justice, and empowerment have continued to be guiding concepts within community psychology.

Community Psychology has outlined a core set of competencies (Dalton & Wolfe, 2012) for practice that may be useful for many future psychologists looking to engage in antiracism. These 18 competencies are organized into 5 categories: foundational principles, community program development and management, community and organizational capacity-building, community and social change, and community research. The foundational principles include **ecological perspectives, empowerment, sociocultural and cross-cultural competence, community inclusion and partnership**, and **ethical, reflective practice**. These themes should now be familiar with you as they have been introduced throughout this book as practices central to antiracism.

Stemming from these foundational principles, we can see additional, specific competencies that center the ability to partner and work with others to better understand and address social injustice and make positive changes. We outline each category of competencies but encourage you to consult the competencies as their specific language may help you identify specific skills or knowledge you may want to pursue as you pursue your profession. The second category, **community program development and management**, includes those abilities that psychologists can use to partner with communities to develop and implement programs to make an identifiable change. The third category, **community and organizing capacity-building**, specifically refers to those abilities that are needed to work in coalition with others and maintain relationships to achieve community-identified goals. The fourth category, **community and social change**, includes those competencies that support bringing together communities to identify common goals, gain power, and work with other leaders to achieve those goals. Lastly, the fifth category, **community research**, describes those abilities to partner with community members to conduct research or evaluate ongoing programs. As a whole, these competencies are a set of concrete skills for community psychologists and others looking to partner directly with impacted communities to transform their environments. We encourage you to seek out resources, such as courses, trainings and professionl development, for those specific competencies that resonate with you.

Applying Antiracism within Psychology

Chapter 1 provides an overview of early career steps for developing an antiracist lens in your profession. These steps can be adapted within the field of psychology, regardless of whether you become a school psychologist, clinical psychologist, or psychometrician. This chapter has outlined particular areas where you may build your understanding but also look to build a network and identify mentors within the field.

In addition to the previous steps outlined, there are critical skills which may be helpful toward developing antiracist approaches in your work. These skills include:

- Asset-based community development
- Power mapping

- Articulating a theory of change
- Reflexivity
- Root cause identification
- Deep Listening
- Creating community around shared goals
- Program and/or community development
- Policy analysis
- Celebrating successes
- Evaluation

One resource toward developing these skills is the Community Tool Box (ctb.ku.edu). This website has been developed by community psychologists and contains step-by-step guides toward developing essential skills for community development. We encourage you to explore the website and search for related modules toward these skills.

These skills can be gained at any point through your career by searching for professional development opportunities. Such opportunities may be present in professional societies related to your specific career or through organizations outside of the field.

Reflect and Practice Activities

Case Study Analysis

Two case studies are included throughout the text. Review these case studies and reflect on the following questions:

- Do you think these projects are addressing systemic racism, why or why not?
- How does the project integrate cultural understandings, critical consciousness, and/or empowerment and resilience, if at all?
- How does the CIP project differ from the Deconstructing Gender-Based Violence project in addressing racism? How do these each reveal different approaches to addressing racism?

Antiracism Audit of Psychological Concepts and Measures

As discussed above, communities of color have largely been absent from the research samples within psychology. This results in both knowledge and assessment tools that, at best, do not reflect the experiences of these communities, and at worst, can be used to perpetuate inequities already faced by communities of color. Reflecting on the samples and sources that underlie the knowledge base for your work, or assessment tools that you use can help you gauge the appropriateness of these concepts and tools for your work. Below we offer the following steps to conduct an antiracism audit of psychological concepts and measures.

1 Identify the concept or assessment tool that you use or are interested in.

For example, if you work in early childhood education you may be interested in classroom quality or assessments related to classroom quality like the Classroom Assessment Scoring System (CLASS) or Assessing Classroom Sociocultural Equity Scale (ACES; Curenton et al., 2019). Alternatively, you may be a counseling psychologist in training interested in understanding trauma and Post-traumatic stress disorder (PTSD) or measures for PTSD.

2 Familiarize yourself with the breadth of literature on the topic or tool.

At this point, you do not need to be saving articles or reading deeply. Instead get a sense for your topic – what are the titles of articles and common questions, who is frequently publishing on this topic, how broad is this topic. Skim articles to see who is commonly cited during introductions and literature review sections.

3 Identify key empirical articles on the topic or recent literature reviews.

After you have familiarized yourself with research on the topic, identify those empirical articles that are commonly used within the field to introduce the topic. See if you can identify a literature review on the topic – the literature review may help identify those central empirical articles on the subject, already contain an analysis of papers in this area, and/or contextualize how the topic addresses racial/ethnic representation.

4 Investigate the racial and ethnic sample of central articles

Consider utilizing a matrix, like the one below, to track the racial/ethnic breakdown of the samples used in the central articles. Jot notes to yourself on how these papers consider the role of race, ethnicity, or racism as related to the topic (Table 2.1).

5 Identify critical empirical articles or commentary on the topic

There may be critical empirical articles which seek to center specific racial or ethnic populations or explore how the topic is understood within communities of color – seek these out. Additionally, skim your search results for commentary articles or introductions to special issues which may include critical perspectives on the topic. Take notes of how these perspectives differ from the central articles.

Table 2.1 Sample matrix to explore racial/ethnic breakdown of samples in empirical articles around a topic of interest

Article Title	Article Authors	Topic Area	Racial/Ethnic Breakdown of Sample	Notes

6 Determine the level to which the existing research is substantially inclusive of communities of color

   Looking across your notes from the central articles and critical articles make a determination in regard to how you feel this topic has included the perspectives of communities of color and/or whether generalizations on the topic can be applied across racial/ethnic groups. Please note that this should be tailored to your specific topic. For example, if you are interested in focusing on wellbeing in Asian families, you might consider how the literature includes specific peoples, like Southeast Asians and South Asian, who are often excluded in the literature (Bernardo et al., 2022).

7 Outline your conclusions

   What have you learned about how your topic includes the experiences of communities of color?

   Reflect on how you may utilize this newfound knowledge. If you find that the topic has not substantively been explored with communities of color, what actions will you take? It may be that you cannot stop using specific assessments, like the DSM criteria for PTSD, but you may be able to incorporate other measures of racial trauma in your practice.

Critical Questions

The reflection and discussion prompts below encourage your critical thinking and engagement with the chapter's content. In response to the prompts below, you can free-write rapid reactions, write longer papers supported by related literature, and/or formulate strategies through small group discussion in class.

1 How has psychological research maintained racism?
2 How can psychologists work with communities of color to create social change?
3 What are two to three skills you would like to develop that can help you undo racism?
4 How can psychologists support individuals interrogating everyday experiences to better understand how racism appears in their own lives?
5 Read the *Apology to People of Color for APA's role in Promoting, Perpetuating, and Failing to Challenge Racism, Racial Discrimination, and Human Hierarchy in the United States* (APA, 2021; https://www.apa.org/about/policy/racism-apology). How does the apology outline next steps for the field of psychology in addressing racism?

Chapter Summary

This chapter introduced you to key concepts to engage in antiracism within psychology. As you consider a potential career in psychology, consider the ways in which you work with others impacted by racism to better understand the histories and structures of injustice and to foster individual and community level change. You have been introduced to key skills and competencies, such as problematization, community-engaged interventions and research, as well as approaches to psychology that can guide your future work, such as liberation psychology. The field of psychology maintains racism through the use of many concepts and measures that have not been developed to capture the experiences of communities of color. As such, antiracism within the field requires deep reflection on existing knowledge and continuous professional growth.

Recommended Resources

The following statements, organizations and other resources may help you deepen your understanding of antiracism in the field of psychology.

- Apology to people of color for APA's role in promoting, perpetuating, and failing to challenge racism, racial discrimination, and human hierarchy in United States: https://www.apa.org/about/policy/racism-apology
- Protecting and Defending our People: Nakni tushka anowa (The Protecting and Defending our People: Nakni tushka anowa (The Warrior's Path) Final Report. APA Division 45 Warrior's Path Warrior's Path) Final Report. APA Division 45 Warrior's Path Presidential Task Force (2020) Presidential Task Force (2020): https://doi.org/10.26077/2en0-6610
- Special Issue of the American Psychologist: Dismantling Racism in the Field of Psychology and Beyond: https://psycnet.apa.org/PsycARTICLES/journal/amp/79/4
- Society for Community Research and Action – Community Psychology, Division 27 of the American Psychological Association: https://scra27.org
- Community Tool Box, a free, easy to read, online resource developed by community psychologists that contains over 300 modules to build skills related to developing community initiatives to solve problems and make social change. The Community Tool Box is available in English, Spanish, Arabic, and Farsi. Learn more: ctb.ku.edu
- Gonzalez, R. & Facilitating Power. (2019). The spectrum of community engagement to ownership. https://movementstrategy.org/wp-content/uploads/2021/08/The-Spectrum-of-Community-Engagement-to-Ownership.pdf

References

Alexander, M. (2012). *The new Jim Crow: Mass incarceration in the age of colorblindness.* The New Press.

American Psychological Association (2020). *Demographics of the U.S. psychology workforce* [interactive data tool]. https://www.apa.org/workforce/data-tools/demographics

American Psychological Association (2021). *Apology to people of color for APA's role in promoting, perpetuating, and failing to challenge racism, racial discrimination and human hierarchy in U.S.* https://www.apa.org/about/policy/racism-apology

Anderson, E. R., & Mayes, L. C. (2010). Race/ethnicity and internalizing disorders in youth: A review. *Clinical Psychology Review, 30*(3), 338–348. https://doi.org/10.1016/j.cpr.2009.12.008

APA Division 45 Warrior's Path Presidential Task Force (2020). Protecting and defending our people: Nakni tushka anowa (The warrior's path) [Final Report]. American Psychological Association Division 45 Society for the Psychological Study of Culture, Ethnicity and Race.

Awad, G. H., Cokley, K. O., Comas-Díaz, L., Hall, G. C. N., & Gone, J. P. (2024). Dismantling racism in the field of psychology and beyond: Introduction to the special issue. *American Psychologist, 79*(4), 477–483. https://doi.org/10.1037/amp0001378

Bernardo, A. B., Mateo, N. J., & Dela Cruz, I. C. (2022). The psychology of well-being in the margins: Voices from and prospects for South Asia and Southeast Asia. *Psychological Studies, 67*(3), 273–280.

Bowers, E. P., Winburn, E. N., Sandoval, A. M., & Clanton, T. (2020). Culturally relevant strengths and positive development in high achieving youth of color. *Journal of Applied Developmental Psychology, 70*, 101182.

Brodsky, A. E., Welsh, E., Carrillo, A., Talwar, G., Scheibler, J., & Butler T. (2011). Between synergy and conflict: Balancing the processes of organizational and individual resilience in an Afghan women's community. *American Journal of Community Psychology, 47*, 217–235. https://doi.org/10.1007/s10464-010-9399-5

Brodsky, A. E., & Cattaneo, L. B. (2013). A transconceptual model of empowerment and resilience: Divergence, convergence and interactions in kindred community concepts. *American Journal of Community Psychology, 52*(3–4), 333–346. https://doi.org/10.1007/s10464-013-9599-x

Buckingham, S. L., Schroeder, T. U., & Hutchinson, J. R. (2023). Elder-led cultural identity program as counterspace at a public university: Narratives on sense of community, empowering settings, and empowerment. *American Journal of Community Psychology, 72*, 32–47. https://doi.org/10.1002/ajcp.12673

Cammarota, J., & Romero, A. (2009). A social justice epistemology and pedagogy for Latina/o students: Transforming public education with participatory action research. *New Directions for Youth Development, 2009*(123), 53–65. https://doi.org/10.1002/yd.314

Castro, M., Expósito-Casas, E., López-Martín, E., Lizasoain, L., Navarro-Asencio, E., & Gaviria, J. L. (2015). Parental involvement on student academic achievement: A meta-analysis. *Educational research review, 14*, 33–46.

Chávez, V., Duran, B., Baker, Q.E., Avila, M. M., & Wallerstein, N. (2003). The dance of race and privilege in community based participatory research. In M. Minkler & N. Wallerstein (Eds.), *Community-based participatory research for health* (pp. 81–97). Jossey-Bass.

Chen, C. Y., Kahanamoku, S. S., Tripati, A., Alegado, R. A., Morris, V. R., Andrade, K., & Hosbey, J. (2022). Meta-research: Systemic racial disparities in funding rates at the National Science Foundation. *eLife, 11*, Article e83071. https://doi.org/10.7554/eLife.83071.

Cummings Center for the History of Psychology (2021). *Examining psychology's contributions to the belief in racial hierarchy and perpetuation of inequality for People of Color in the United States.* Cummings Center for the History of Psychology.

Curenton, S. M., Iruka, I. U., Humphries, M., Jensen, M., Durden, T., Rochester, S. E., Sims, J., Whittaker, J., & Kinzie, M. (2019). Validity for the Assessing Classroom Sociocultural Equity Scale (ACSES) in early childhood classrooms. *Early Education and Development, 31*(2), 284–303. https://doi.org/10.1080/10409289.2019.1611331

Dalton, J., & Wolfe, S. (2012). Education connection and the community practitioner: Competencies for community psychology practice. *The Community Psychologist, 45*(4), 7–14.

Diemer, M. A., Rapa, L. J., Voight, A. M., & McWhirter, E. H. (2016). Critical consciousness: A developmental approach to addressing marginalization and oppression. *Child Development Perspectives, 10*(4), 216–221.

Epstein, J. L. (2010). School/family/community partnerships: Caring for the children we share. *Phi delta kappan, 92*(3), 81–96.

Fan, X., & Chen, M. (2001). Parental involvement and students' academic achievement: A meta-analysis. *Educational Psychology Review, 13*, 1–22.

Feng, X., Harkness, S., Super, C. M., Welles, B., Rios Bermudez, M., Bonichini, S., Moscardino, U., & Zylicz, P. O. (2020). Parents' concepts of the successful school child in seven western cultures. *New Directions for Child and Adolescent Development, 170*, 143–170. https://doi.org/10.1002/cad.20337

Fernández, J. S. (2024). A mujerista liberation psychology perspective on testimonio to cultivate decolonial healing. In *Feminist liberation practice with Latinx women* (pp. 9–34). Routledge. https://doi.org/10.1080/02703149.2022.2095101

Fox, D., Prilleltensky, I., & Austin, S. (2009). Critical psychology for social justice: Concerns and dilemmas. In D. Fox, I. Prilleltensky, & S. Austin (Eds.), *Critical psychology: An introduction* (2nd ed., pp. 3–19). Sage Publications Ltd.

Freire, P. (1970). *Pedagogy of the oppressed*. Seabury Press.

Fuller, B., & García Coll, C. (2010). Learning from Latinos: Contexts, families, and child development in motion. *Developmental Psychology, 46*(3), 559–565.

Ginther, D. K., Schaffer, W. T., Schnell, J., Masimore, B., Liu, F., Haak, L. L., & Kington, R. (2011). Race, ethnicity, and NIH research awards. *Science, 333*, 1015–1019. https://doi.org/10.1126/science.1196783

Ginwright, S. (2018). The future of healing: Shifting from trauma informed care to healing centered engagement. Kinship Carers Victoria. https://ginwright.medium.com/the-future-of-healing-shifting-from-trauma-informed-care-to-healing-centered-engagement-634f557ce69c

Gómez, J. M., Caño, A., & Baltes, B. B. (2021). Who are we missing? Examining the Graduate Record Examination quantitative score as a barrier to admission into psychology doctoral programs for capable ethnic minorities. *Training and Education in Professional Psychology, 15*(3), 211–218. https://doi.org/10.1037/tep0000336

Gonzalez, R. & Facilitating Power. (2019). *The spectrum of community engagement to ownership*. https://movementstrategy.org/wp-content/uploads/2021/08/The-Spectrum-of-Community-Engagement-to-Ownership.pdf

Guthrie, R. (1976). *Even the rat was white: A historical view of psychology*. Harper & Row.

Hagey, R. S. (1997). The use and abuse of participatory action research. *Chronic Diseases in Canada, 18*(1), 1–4.

Harkness, S., Super, C. M., Bermúdez, M. R., Moscardino, U., Rha, J. H., Mavridis, C. J., ... Zylicz, P. O. (2010). Parental ethnotheories of children's learning. In D. F. Lancy, J. Bock, & S. Gaskins (Eds.), *The anthropology of learning in childhood* (pp. 65–81). AltaMira Press.

Henrich, J., Heine, S. J., & Norenzayan, A. (2010). The weirdest people in the world. *Behavioral and Brain Sciences, 33*(2–3), 61–235. https://doi.org/10.1017/S0140525X0 999152X

Hergenrather, K. C., Rhodes, S. D., Bardhoshi, G., & Pula, S. (2009). Photovoice as community-based participatory research: A qualitative review. *American Journal of Health Behavior, 33*(6), 686–698. https://doi.org/10.5993/AJHB.33.6.6

Hoppe, T. A., Litovitz, A., Willis, K. A., Meseroll, R. A., Perkins, M. J., Hitchins, B. I., Davis, A. F., Lauer, M. S., Valantine, H. A., Anderson, J. M., & Santangelo, G. M. (2019). Topic choice contributes to the lower rate of NIH awards to African-American/Black scientists. *Science Advances, 5*(10), Article eaaw7238. https://doi.org/10.1126/sciadv.aaw7238

Kelly, J.G. (1986), Context and process: An ecological view of the interdependence of practice and research. *American Journal of Community Psychology, 14,* 573–579.

Krueger-Henney, P. (2014). It's not just a method! The epistemic and political work of young people's lifeworlds at the school–prison nexus. In E. R. Meiners & M. T. Winn (Eds.), *Education and incarceration* (pp. 108–133). Routledge.

Lareau, A. (2011). *Unequal childhoods: class, race, and family life.* University of California Press.

Lord, J., & Hutchinson, P. (1993). The process of empowerment: Implications for theory and practice. *Canadian Journal of Community Mental Health, 12*(1), 5–22.

Lundy, P., & McGovern, M. (2006). Action research, community 'truth-telling' and post-conflict transition in the North of Ireland. *Action Research, 4*(1), 49–64. https://doi.org/10.1177/1476750306060542

Lykes, M. B., & Scheib, H. (2018). Visual methodologies and participatory action research: Performing women's community-based health promotion in post-Katrina New Orleans. *Participatory visual methodologies in global public health, 11*(5–6), 222–241. https://doi.org/10.1080/17441692.2016.1170180

Martín-Baró, I. (1996). *Writings for a liberation psychology.* Harvard University Press.

Maton, K. I. (2008). Empowering community settings: Agents of individual development, community betterment, and positive social change. *American Journal of Community Psychology, 41,* 4–21. https://doi.org/10.1007/s10464-007-9148-6

McKay, S. Veale, A., Worthen, M., Wessells, M., Banya, G., Borbo, S., Wawa-Brown, C., Gbegba, V., Geedah, D., James, E., Kerwgie, A., Laruni, E., Marah, A., Neema, S., Okema, F., Onyango, G., Onyango, P., Sayndee, D., Single D., & Beresford Weekes, S. (2010). Community-based reintegration of war-affected young mothers: Participatory Action Research (PAR) in Liberia, Sierra Leone & Northern Uganda. www.PARGirlMothers.com

McLaughlin, K. A., Hilt, L. M., & Nolen-Hoeksema, S. (2007). Racial/ethnic differences in internalizing and externalizing symptoms in adolescents. *Journal of Abnormal Child Psychology,* 35, 801–816. https://doi.org/10.1007/s10802-007-9128-1.

McWayne, C. M., Melzi, G., Schick, A. R., Kennedy, J. L., & Mundt, K. (2013). Defining family engagement among Latino Head Start parents: A mixed-methods measurement development study. *Early Childhood Research Quarterly, 28*(3), 593–607. https://doi.org/10.1016/j.ecresq.2013.03.008

McWayne, C. M., Melzi, G., Limlingan, M. C., & Schick, A. (2016). Ecocultural patterns of family engagement among low-income Latino families of preschool children. *Developmental Psychology, 52*(7), 1088.

McWayne, C. M., Doucet, F., & Mistry, J. (2019). Family-school partnerships in ethnocultural communities: Reorienting Conceptual frameworks, research methods, and intervention efforts by rotating our lens. In C. M. McWayne, F. Doucet, & S. M. Sheridan (Eds.), *Ethnocultural Diversity and the Home-to-School Link* (pp.1–18), Springer Cham.

Minkler, M. (2004). Ethical challenges for the "outside" researcher in community-based participatory research. *Health Education & Behavior, 31*(6), 684–697. https://doi.org/10.1177/1090198104269566

Montero, M. (2009). Methods for liberation: Critical consciousness in action. In M. Montero & C. C. Sonn (Eds.), *Psychology of liberation: Theory and applications* (pp. 73–91). Springer Science+Business Media, LLC. https://doi.org/10.1007/978-0-387-85784-8_4

Nelson, G. B., & Prilleltensky, I. (2005). Organizational and community interventions. In *Community psychology: In pursuit of liberation and well-being* (pp. 186–210). Palgrave Macmillan.

Norsworthy, K. L., & Khuankaew, O. (2004). Women of Burma speak out: Workshops to deconstruct gender-based violence and build systems of peace and justice. *Journal for Specialists in Group Work, 29*(3), 259–283.

Page, C. (2013). Kindred collective: Cara Page. Healing Collective Trauma. https://kindredsouthernhjcollective.org/what-is-healing-justice/.

Rappaport, J. (1981). In praise of paradox: A social policy of empowerment over prevention. *American Journal of Community Psychology, 9*(1), 1–25. https://doi.org/10.1007/BF00896357

Rodriquez, E. J., Livaudais-Toman, J., Gregorich, S. E., Jackson, J. S., Nápoles, A. M., & Pérez-Stable, E. J. (2018). Relationships between allostatic load, unhealthy behaviors, and depressive disorder in US adults, 2005–2012 NHANES. *Preventive Medicine, 110*, 9–15. https://doi.org/10.1016/j.ypmed.2018.02.002.

Rutter, M. D. M. (1993). Resilience: Some conceptual considerations. *Journal of Adolescent Health, 14*(8), 626–631.

Scarpa, M. P., & Trickett, E. J. (May 12, 2022). Translating ecology: Similarities and differences in the ecological images of Bronfenbrenner and Kelly. *Translational Issues in Psychological Science, 8*(2), 185–196. https://dx. doi.org/10.1037/tps0000315

Steinberg, L., Lamborn, S. D., Dornbusch, S. M., & Darling, N. (1992). Impact of parenting practices on adolescent achievement: Authoritative parenting, school involvement, and encouragement to succeed. *Child Development, 63*(5), 1266–1281.

Syed, M., Santos, C., Yoo, H. C., & Juang, L. P. (2018). Invisibility of racial/ethnic minorities in developmental science: Implications for research and institutional practices. *American Psychologist, 73*(6), 812–816. https://doi.org/10.1037/amp0000294

Teo, T. (2015). Critical psychology: A geography of intellectual engagement and resistance. *American Psychologist, 70*(3), 243–254. https://doi.org/10.1037/a0038727

Wallerstein, N., & Duran, B. (2010). Community-based participatory research contributions to intervention research: the intersection of science and practice to improve health equity. *American Journal of Public Health, 100*(S1), S40–S46.

Wallerstein, N. (2021). Engage for equity: Advancing the fields of community-based participatory research and community-engaged research in community psychology and the social sciences. *American Journal of Community Psychology, 67*(3/4), 251–255. https://doi.org/10.1002/ajcp.12530

Watts, R. J., Williams, N. C., & Jagers, R. J. (2003). Sociopolitical development. *American Journal of Community Psychology, 31*(1–2), 185–194. https://doi.org/10.1023/A:1023091024140.

Weisner, T. S. (2002). Ecocultural Understanding of Children's Developmental Pathways. *Human Development, 45*(4), 275–281.

Chapter 3

Antiracist Developmental Teaching in PK-12 Education

Introduction

Assuming you are reading this book because you are interested in specifically *developmental antiracist perspectives on PK-12 teaching*, it is essential to recognize that an important part of the foundation of antiracist teaching lies *within the teachers themselves*. Research supports that one of the most impactful antiracist actions a teacher can take begins with critical self-reflection and personal change (Utt & Tochluk, 2020). While many educators are eager to dive into actionable strategies for the classroom, meaningful antiracist educational transformation is rooted in deeply in personal work.

Developing **critical consciousness**, an ongoing, evolving awareness of one's own biases, assumptions, and positionalities, is not just some preliminary step to outward action; it is a continuous process that directly shapes one's ability to effect change with students (Suzuki et al., 2023). Teachers cannot nurture critical awareness in their students without cultivating it in themselves, which demands a commitment to understanding and questioning the social and political structures surrounding education (Ladson-Billings, 1995). This concept of interconnectedness is similar to the airplane safety guideline that advises passengers to secure their own oxygen masks before assisting others. In the same way, teachers must recognize the necessity of addressing their own biases and positionalities to authentically support their students in a world that is far from race-neutral.

A recurring theme in this chapter will be to examine the education system through a developmental lens, locating teachers and their *roles within the system* and then *making connections between the system and individual choices within a teacher's control*. This focus on self-awareness is not about navel-gazing; it is a practical necessity. In the busy, intense world of PK-12 education, there are numerous moving parts, many needs, and constant demands, with a continuous call to look away and be "student-centered" (a familiar educational buzzword!) from administration, teacher education programs, and, not least of all, teachers' own hearts.

DOI: 10.4324/9781003374176-4

Part of this self-awareness is considering how traditional developmental theories have been applied in educational contexts. Developmental theories of some sort often guide what teachers think of as "true" about the nature of teaching and learning and guide the ways that curriculum is written (and then taught), and what educators believe to be the *best practices* in general for interacting with students in their care. Teachers bring developmental frameworks with them into the classroom through not only the way curriculum is designed, but also in their everyday sense-making as they move through their work. Foundational theories – such as those by Erikson, Piaget, Vygotsky, and even Bronfenbrenner – are often treated as universally applicable in education. However, the way these theories are applied in curriculum and pedagogy frequently lack explicit considerations of the *specifics of context,* and of specific interest of this book, for examining child development through a racial lens that accounts for privilege and oppression (Syed et al., 2018). Shaped by historical and limited perspectives, general theories often overlook the systemic factors influencing marginalized students and fail to address the impacts of racism and cultural bias within contemporary educational spaces (Iruka et al., 2022). This chapter aims to prompt critical reflection and a reconceptualization around some of these limitations.

Teachers are undoubtedly there for the kids. However, the reality is that *teachers teach who they are.* If teachers don't reflect on it, their personal and culturally shaped ideas about what makes a "good" student can end up defining classroom rules and expectations, often just reflecting themselves (Reyes & Aronson, 2022). When the teacher's identity, experience, or worldview does not reflect that of the students in their class, this can create challenges. For example, research shows that identity mismatch contributes to disproportionate discipline rates for students of color, the lack of diverse representation in school libraries, and teachers' biases related to race, gender, socioeconomic status, and language background, which shape their perceptions of students' experiences at both school and home (Baines et al., 2018; Duane & Winninghoff, 2023; Matthews, 2021; Wood et al., 2020). Teachers may *intend* to be "student-centered" in their approach to curriculum and pedagogy, but without systemic awareness of the dominant norms they may unconsciously reinforce, an understanding of how their positionality shapes their view of everyday interactions and decisions, or recognition of the impacts of racism within education, they may inadvertently undermine their own good intentions (Herrera, 2021; Duane & Winninghoff, 2023).

In this chapter, we will explore education as a developmental context and the antiracist potential of the teacher's role within it. We will emphasize why applying antiracist developmental science is crucial for understanding what is happening in the field of education, particularly the ways in which teacher and student interactions can either *perpetuate or challenge systemic racism.* This reframing of teaching beyond individual *teacher-student interactions* emphasizes the broader, *contextualized role of a teacher,* highlighting their influence as mediators of meaning and designers of educational environments. We will discuss key issues such as *classroom management practices*, *curriculum choices*, and *school policies* that impact racial equity. By examining these aspects, we aim to provoke thought, challenge assumptions, and inspire a deeper commitment to viewing the teaching profession through an antiracist developmental lens.

This chapter's key features include:

- Foundations of Teacher Identity
- An Introduction to the (White) Zones of Proximal Development
- Establishing a Critical Reflective Practice
- Applying Antiracist Developmental Frameworks in PK-12 Contexts
- Reflect and Practice Activities
- Recommended Resources

Foundations of Teacher Identity

Why do people become teachers? It may not surprise you that many pre-service and early career educators consistently cite their desire to "make a difference" as motivation for choosing this career path. The aspiration to positively impact the lives of children and adolescents is a significant driving force behind the decision to enter the classroom (Fray & Gore, 2018). The idea that "helping" is a key part of the job description of being a teacher is one that has been communicated in a variety of ways to most of us in society over the course of our lives. It is a message that would have been hard to miss.

Teachers are frequently referred to as those who have the potential to be "saviors" in our society, depicted in the media as battling against overwhelming odds, sometimes equipped with little more than their dedication and moral fortitude. Such portrayals can be deeply appealing, painting teachers as heroes who, in some form, have the potential to rescue their students from various challenging circumstances. This imagery is echoed in public discourse, where teachers are often lauded for their sacrifices and portrayed as selfless martyrs dedicated to their noble mission (Goldin et al., 2021; Duane & Winninghoff, 2023). Cultural representations both mirror and shape our collective understanding of what it means to be a teacher, giving readily accessible examples of popular messages about teachers' *saviorism*.

Many tend to view teaching through its impact at the **individual or interpersonal level**, focusing on the direct relationships between teachers and their students and the day-to-day, immediate, observable effects on learning. While not untrue, narrowing the view of teaching to this space limits the ability to see the broader **systemic context** in which teaching operates, including how individual teachers can perpetuate or *challenge societal inequities* through their educational practices in the workspace (Freire, 1970; Ladson-Billings, 1995). In reality, beginning teachers need both the opportunity and sustained guidance in developing their ability to shift their perspectives (or change "lenses"), in order to view the larger, long-lasting societal impact of their teaching (Herrera, 2021).

In addition to the focus on individual saviors, there's a perennial barrier for antiracist development and the teacher: the *societal taboo* around openly discussing race and racism in meaningful, nuanced ways. This silence leads to a widespread lack of **developmental racial literacy**, or the ability to recognize, understand, and critically engage with how race and racism shape human development across contexts, affecting everyone within the educational system, from teachers and administrators to students and parents (Reyes & Aronson, 2022). When racial issues are avoided by educators, curriculum standards, or school policies, the system reinforces racist ideologies, allowing teachers to continue to *participate in socialization around biased understandings of race* that may remain unexamined throughout their careers. This surface-level avoidance doesn't reduce racism; rather, it entrenches racial biases within educators, limiting their capacity to address race and equity meaningfully in all aspects of their work – from classroom interactions to policy implementation and professional relationships (Bonilla-Silva, 2021).

For instance, teachers may feel that addressing race and systemic inequity falls outside their role or expertise, viewing it as a sensitive topic best avoided to prevent controversy with parents or the larger community. Yet, when teachers view their work solely within the confines of individual classrooms or isolated actions, the broader systemic impact of their professional choices can be obscured. Consequently, this cycle of misunderstanding and reluctance perpetuates itself within the profession, creating educational spaces where biases are reinforced across generations (Olsen, 2015).

The connections between the *larger systems and the interactions at the classroom level* are not easily recognized when just thinking about teachers as individuals who are working with their students in a decontextualized way. This concept can be illustrated by the traditional South Asian story of the "Blind Men and the Elephant," which appears in Jain, Buddhist, and Hindu texts (Ireland, 1997; Sarma, 2000; Umasvati, 1994). In this story, a group of blind men each touch a different part of an elephant – one touches the trunk, another the leg, another the ear. Each forms a different interpretation of what they are encountering, based only on the part they can feel, without seeing the whole animal. Their limited, individual experiences create a fragmented and incomplete understanding of the elephant.

Similarly, when teachers view their roles only through the lens of individual classrooms or isolated actions, the larger, *systemic impact of their work* can be obscured. Consequently, the transformative potential of education to address and dismantle structural inequalities in society as a whole is frequently underestimated or misunderstood. Greater awareness and integration of *systemic perspectives in teaching practices* are essential, enabling educators to recognize their contributions within a larger *developmental context of socialization* (Kishimoto, 2018). In doing so, they can more intentionally challenge or dismantle structures that perpetuate inequities around race, power, and identity, rather than unknowingly reinforce them (Olsen, 2015). By seeing the "whole elephant" – this larger systemic landscape – teachers can more consciously align their practices with an antiracist vision. That is, if they are ready to commit to learning about and working to embody what it means to be an "antiracist teacher." So, if teachers aren't individual saviors, out there saving all of the kids, then what are they? What should they be? For that matter, what is teaching?

Teachers Teach Who They Are

Many people assume that teachers primarily learn how to teach through their preparation programs. What future teachers need to also deeply consider is that, long before formal preparation even begins, they have also been internalizing countless messages about what it means to be a teacher. They have actively participated in a lifelong socialization process, making sense of these messages as students themselves, learning indirectly from the teachers they observed and the educational environments they experienced (Beauchamp & Thomas, 2009; Rogoff, 2003). Teaching is one of the few professions that nearly everyone has a deeply personal connection to in some way; nearly everyone has been a student and has spent years within the walls of schools (Olsen, 2015). This immersion creates a *foundation of personal memories and assumptions* about education that teachers carry with them, often unconsciously, as they develop their professional identities (Beauchamp & Thomas, 2009).

In reality, most future teachers come to the field loaded with memories related to teaching and learning based on years of their own direct experiences in the classroom as students themselves (Olsen, 2015). These memories encompass not only academic but also social experiences around learning, shaped by active engagement with the cultural, familial, and societal influences they were exposed to over time (Beauchamp & Thomas 2009). These factors interact with each individual's unique identities – such as race, gender, socioeconomic background, and language – alongside their personal values, beliefs, and worldviews. Together, these elements form what is known as **positionality**: the distinct positions from which each person views and interprets the world at any particular moment and in any particular context. Positionality reflects how one's social identity and lived experiences influence both personal and professional perspectives, making it a critical factor in shaping how future teachers *understand and engage with all aspects of their work*: from interactions with students of varied backgrounds, identities, and learning needs, to relationships with families, the interpretation of the curriculum, classroom space, instructional tasks, and professional connections. Positionality shapes teachers' understanding of their roles, impacting how they approach classroom dynamics, engage families, collaborate with colleagues, and navigate the educational environment as a whole (Herrera, 2021; Milner, 2010).

Developmental research consistently highlights the significant role of the teacher in shaping educational outcomes for students (; Bonilla-Silva & Embrick, 2008; Rogoff, 2003; Vygotsky, 1978). Teachers' perception, shaped by their own positionalities, guide their reactions and responses to what they observe and experience daily in the classroom. This is crucial to understand from the outset because teachers *mediate learning* and exert considerable control over classroom environments – whether consciously or unconsciously, and whether they fully understand their influence or not (Herrera, 2021). For instance, the way teachers and students interact is vital in shaping how race, a social construct, is understood to begin with and how (anti)racism is either perpetuated or challenged. As *facilitators of learning,* teachers play a significant role in guiding many of these interactions, both consciously and unconsciously, throughout the course of everyday interactions at school (Herrera, 2021).

Extending Vygotsky's Zone of Proximal Development

To provide a strong developmental foundation, we will begin by *revisiting a well-known developmental concept* that continues to inform many educators' foundational understanding of the workings of teaching and learning itself: Vygotsky's Zone of Proximal Development (Vygotsky, 1978). We will analyze its limitations when traditionally applied, and reconceptualize the ZPD within a socio-cultural and specifically antiracist context, by critically *extending* it to the "White" Zones of Proximal Development (Leonardo & Manning, 2017).

Lev Vygotsky's **Zone of Proximal Development (ZPD)** is a foundational concept in developmental and educational psychology that still remains highly influential in contemporary educational practices. Vygotsky's work, originating in the early twentieth-century Soviet Union, has been pivotal in understanding how social interactions drive cognitive development. His theories emphasize that learning is inherently a social process, and this understanding continues to shape modern educational strategies and frameworks (Vygotsky, 1978) (Figure 3.1).

In PK-12 teaching, Vygotsky's ZPD is not just some distant theoretical construct but is an idea that is integrated into the very way that teachers understand the process of learning, and their role in that process. It shows up in one way or another on a daily basis. When you walk into a classroom, whether it's a preschool or a high school, whether anyone in the room is even aware of it or not, the principles of the ZPD are at work.

For instance, when a teacher helps a student solve a math problem by noticing what a student knows (and does not know yet) and then provides just enough hints and guidance to nudge them toward being able to find the solution for themselves, they are operating within the student's ZPD. The teacher is identifying what the student can do with help and is being responsive in that real-time moment, **scaffolding** the learning process to promote problem-solving skills in the student that ultimately leads to their learning. This practice is so ingrained

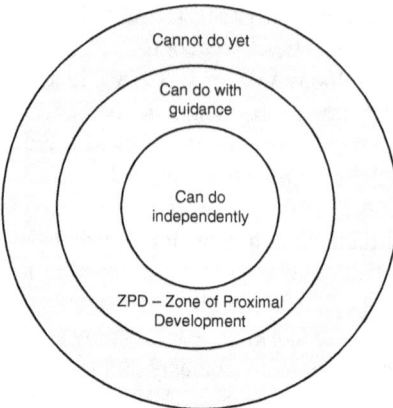

Figure 3.1 Traditional Zone of Proximal Development.

in teaching practices that it often goes unrecognized as a direct application of Vygotsky's theory (Vygotsky, 1978).

The pervasiveness of the ZPD in education means that it has become a given underlying assumption in how we approach teaching and learning. For example, *differentiated instruction*, where lessons are tailored to the varying abilities of students, is rooted in the understanding that each student has a unique ZPD. *Collaborative learning activities*, such as *project-based learning* and pair work, also draw heavily on the idea that students can learn from social interactions. These strategies are designed to stretch students' capabilities by placing them in socially interactive settings where they can acquire new skills and knowledge when combined with the support and knowledgeable of others (Vygotsky, 1978).

Key Concepts of the ZPD

More Knowledgeable Other (MKO): The MKO is an individual or resource with greater knowledge or skill in a particular area than the learner, such as a teacher, peer, or even educational materials. The MKO role is flexible and dynamic, shifting based on the context and task. The MKO provides guidance and scaffolding to support the learner's progression through their ZPD (Vygotsky, 1978).

Scaffolding: This term refers to the temporary support provided by the MKO, which is gradually removed as the learner gains independence. Think of the scaffolding that is used to support a building while it is under construction. Scaffolding can include various instructional strategies such as prompting, modeling, and feedback. The goal is to help the learner achieve tasks they could not accomplish alone (Wood et al., 1976).

Internalization: Vygotsky posited that cognitive functions are initially mediated through social interactions and then internalized by the learner. This process transforms external activities into internal cognitive processes, enabling learners to perform tasks independently that they initially could not (Vygotsky, 1978).

Application of ZPD in Education

Vygotsky's ZPD has been applied extensively in educational settings to organize thinking around teaching and learning:

Differentiated Instruction: Teachers use their understanding of their students' ZPDs to provide differentiated instruction tailored to individual learning needs. This approach aims to responsively challenge and support all students in their development (Tomlinson, 2014).

Collaborative Learning: Group work and peer tutoring leverage the principles of ZPD by allowing students to assist each other in learning tasks, expanding their individual ZPDs through social interaction and shared knowledge (Johnson et al., 1998).

Formative Assessment: Teachers use formative assessments to gauge students' current levels of understanding and to responsively tailor instruction that targets their ZPDs. This helps in their ability to discern and provide the right level of challenge and support (Black & Wiliam, 1998).

The White Zones of Proximal Development

While Vygotsky's ZPD provides a model for understanding learning in general, it does not make explicit the racial dynamics that critically shape today's sociocultural contexts. This limitation becomes particularly evident when considering the United States, where racialized power imbalances are embedded within educational systems. To address these gaps, Leonardo and Manning (2017) introduced the concept of **White Zones of Proximal Development** (WZPD), which incorporates critical race perspectives to highlight how Whiteness operates as a dominant racial and cultural force within educational settings. WZPD reinterprets Vygotsky's theory to center race as a pervasive influence on educational interactions, practices, and policies, making racial dynamics a focus of educational analysis (Gillborn, 2005; Leonardo, 2013; Matias, 2015; Mills, 1997; Figure 3.2).

The WZPD framework serves as a tool for examining how structures of power, rooted in Whiteness, shape both individual and collective development in U.S. schools. By focusing on Whiteness as an influential "sign system," the WZPD emphasizes that certain cultural norms, values, and expectations associated with Whiteness mediate how educational content is delivered, interpreted, and internalized by both teachers and students. For instance, curriculum choices, classroom management styles, and disciplinary practices are often unconsciously aligned with dominant White cultural standards, potentially marginalizing students who are not White. This framing allows educators to consider

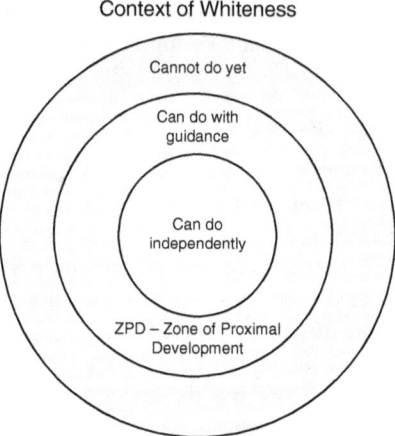

Figure 3.2 Whites Zone of Proximal Development.

how seemingly neutral educational practices can perpetuate racial biases when situated within a larger hegemonic social and historical context.

Key Concepts of the WZPD

Whiteness as a Sign System: Leonardo and Manning describe Whiteness as a pervasive signaling that shapes social interactions and learning experiences in much the same way Vygotsky's *concept of language mediates thought and behavior.* For example, values such as *individualism, competition,* and *"standard"* English language proficiency often become the hidden *curriculum*—or unwritten standards and norms—in schools, shaping how students' abilities are perceived and how knowledge is conveyed (Leonardo & Manning, 2017).

Racial Mediation: Central to the WZPD framework is the idea that racial dynamics mediate educational interactions. For instance, a White teacher may unconsciously align with cultural norms that reflect their own positionality, unintentionally reinforcing biases that marginalize students who do not share those norms. This can manifest in assumptions about "proper" behavior, basic ideas around what makes a student "smart," and learning styles, all of which are often seen through a lens shaped by Whiteness. Such biases may lead to a narrowed view of student potential, disproportionately affecting students of color (Leonardo & Manning, 2017).

Critical Consciousness in Teachers: Developing critical consciousness around the dominant influence of Whiteness is crucial for educators seeking to enact antiracist teaching practices. This means not only recognizing how Whiteness mediates learning but also examining how teachers' own racial identities and positionalities interact with Whiteness (this includes *internalized oppression* for teachers with marginalized identities) to shape their practices. By becoming aware of these dynamics, teachers can begin to actively dismantle inequitable norms within their classrooms, engaging students in ways that validate their identities and experiences (Leonardo & Manning, 2017).

White Teachers, White Zones

The vast majority of public school teachers in the United States have been, and to this day still are, White (Ahmad & Boser, 2014). The need for WZPD becomes evident when considering the persistent opportunity gaps and disproportionate disciplinary actions that impact students of color in U.S. schools (Wood et al., 2020). The traditional ZPD, while effective for understanding the basic process of social learning, may inadvertently contribute to these issues if not adapted to recognize the ways in which White cultural norms dominate educational experiences (Leonardo & Manning, 2017). For example, a classroom policy enforcing "English only" privileges centering monolingual students who speak standard English while marginalizing multilingual students, as well as those who speak other varieties of English, such as African American Vernacular English (AAVE). Not only is such a policy racist, but it is also misaligned with current developmental research on linguistic development, including findings on translanguaging and the cognitive and academic benefits of multilingualism (Garcia & Kleifgen, 2020; Garcia et al., 2017). Similarly, disciplinary policies rooted in respect for authority without questioning may unfairly impact students from cultural backgrounds where open discussion and critical inquiry are encouraged. Research shows that BIPOC students are disproportionately disciplined compared to their White peers, often for subjective offenses like "defiance" or "disruptiveness," which can reflect biases linked to racial stereotypes (Herrera, 2021). For instance, a Black student might be seen as "threatening" or "aggressive" in situations where a White student exhibiting similar behavior might be perceived as "assertive" or "energetic" (Herrera, 2021).

The WZPD framework provides teachers with a tool with which to view, analyze, and adjust these policies, encouraging reflection on how Whiteness shapes their expectations and practices. By expanding Vygotsky's ZPD to include critical perspectives on race, WZPD empowers educators to create learning environments that are not only developmentally appropriate but also race-visible. This shift not only benefits students of color but also cultivates a more equitable educational experience for all students.

Establishing a Critical Reflective Practice

Building an antiracist identity begins with cultivating a reflective practice that allows teachers to critically examine their beliefs, biases, and assumptions. Building on the Early Career Steps for Developing an Antiracist Lens in Your Profession and Antiracist Praxis Model introduced in Chapter 1, this section highlights reflection as a continual process.

Critical Reflection for Teachers

Reflective practice requires teachers to regularly question their decisions, interactions, and assumptions, going beyond basic self-assessment to critically analyze how their personal beliefs and positionalities influence student interactions and classroom dynamics. For instance, a teacher recognizing a recurring bias in their expectations of students would then enact deep reflection to gain the complex understanding of the many interacting systems and perspectives needed needed for corrective action. This practice fosters greater self-awareness and intentionality, enabling teachers to cultivate a classroom that promotes equity and inclusivity.

The *Early Career Steps for Developing an Antiracist Lens in Your Profession* offer beginning teachers a structured path toward cultivating an antiracist identity, one grounded in critical reflection and a commitment to equity in teaching practices. Teachers direct attention toward building *foundational awareness*, noticing the *biases and structural inequities* within educational systems. As these come into focus, they examine the influences in various *ecological systems*, recognizing how personal interactions and institutional policies shape students' experiences and impact classroom practices. This reflection extends to their own identities, as teachers assess how their social positions and potential biases might influence their perceptions and interactions with students.

With this awareness, teachers begin to apply an antiracist lens *across teaching activities*, actively identifying inequities and transforming curriculum design and classroom management to better support all students. *Engaging with diverse stakeholders* – students, families, and colleagues – provides insight into the broader social dynamics that affect student lives, fostering a more inclusive environment. *Mentorship and professional networks* play a critical role, offering support and guidance as teachers navigate antiracist work. Through *continuous professional development*, teachers stay updated on evolving practices, integrating new insights into their approaches. As they implement antiracist practices, regular reflection allows teachers to *adapt based on feedback*, ensuring their teaching evolves with their understanding. Recognizing that this journey is ongoing, they commit to continual growth and adaptation, *viewing antiracist work as a lifelong commitment*.

Building on this foundation, beginning teachers must also develop *racial and equity literacies* to navigate the complexities of race, power, and privilege in education. Beyond cultural awareness, these literacies equip teachers to critically examine their own positionalities and the systemic forces at play in education. Through these lenses, educators can better recognize and challenge the impacts of systemic racism, working consciously to create inclusive and equitable learning environments.

Racial Literacy for Teachers

Racial literacy for teachers involves cultivating *a deep understanding of race as a social construct, including the historical, social, and political forces that have shaped racial dynamics*. This literacy is about more than simply discussing race in the classroom with others – it's about ensuring that teachers *themselves* understand what race is *and is not* in complex and nuanced ways, how racism functions on systemic and individual levels, and the impact of racial identity on all students (including White students).

For example, a racially literate teacher avoids using "culture" as a vague or intended euphemistic proxy for "race." Such imprecision can obscure important discussions about race and its unique role in shaping educational inequities. If a racially literate teacher is talking specifically about race, they will say so. Additionally, many beginning White teachers (not exclusively) may not have had explicit education in understanding that White people also have a race and culture, which can affect their teaching. In the U.S., where the majority of teachers are White, many have been socialized into racial silence, meaning that discussing race, particularly Whiteness, is often considered inappropriate, impolite, or even taboo. This socialization is so deeply internalized that many White teachers may not even recognize it as a form of avoidance, nor have they interrogated why race has been treated as something to be ignored or downplayed.

Developing racial literacy requires unlearning this silence and understanding that, at least in the context of the United States, Whiteness carries unearned privilege within a broader structure of racial hierarchy. While acknowledging this may feel uncomfortable for everyone (and can be met with particular discomfort by those who identify as White), it is an important step in recognizing one's own role within these dynamics and working toward more just and equitable educational practices. Concrete steps toward building racial literacy might include:

- **Learning about the history of race and racism** in the United States and globally to understand the origins and evolution of racial categories and hierarchies.
- **Understanding White supremacy as a systemic construct** that goes beyond individual prejudice, influencing institutional practices and policies that favor White individuals and norms.
- **Avoiding euphemisms or coded language** when discussing race or systemic racism. For instance, instead of saying "diverse backgrounds" when they specifically mean students of color (or, for that matter, using "students of color" when they specifically mean "Black"), or "bad schools" when they specifically mean schools situated in historically redlined neighborhoods that are filled with students of color, etc., teachers would be more precise by naming relevant racial or structural inequities.

- **Learn about White racial identity development.** A racially literate teacher understands that *Whiteness is a racialized experience* and that White students, like all students, develop their racial identities within a broader social and historical context. They seek to understand what *healthy White racial identity development* is and can be—both for their students and for themselves (if White). This work is not only about individual growth but about *collective healing*, recognizing that *we don't heal until we all heal* (Helms, 2020).

A racially literate teacher might also learn to recognize their own biases, particularly regarding **colorblind racism approaches**, which claim not to "see" race but, in reality, contribute to ignoring systemic inequities and maintaining the status quo. This "not seeing" is not neutral, it reinforces existing power structures by dismissing the lived realities of people across racial groups (Turner, 2019; Syed et al., 2018). Through the development of racial literacy, teachers learn to challenge these neutral-seeming, racist approaches by acknowledging the contextualized experiences of all racial groups and understanding how their own racial identities impact their perspectives and everyday interactions with others.

Equity Literacy for Teachers

Equity literacy equips beginning teachers with the skills to identify and actively address biases embedded within educational practices, curricula, and school policies (Gorski & Swalwell, 2015). This literacy empowers teachers to critically evaluate how norms and policies might advantage or disadvantage students based on race, socioeconomic status, and other identity factors.

For instance, a teacher developing equity literacy might notice disparities in disciplinary actions within their school, where students of color may face harsher or more frequent punishment for the same behaviors exhibited by White students. Developing equity literacy would prompt the teacher to question these disciplinary practices, understanding them as products of embedded racial biases rather than isolated incidents (Gorski & Swalwell, 2015). A teacher with strong equity literacy might also advocate for restorative practices rather than punitive measures, recognizing that traditional disciplinary policies often reproduce systemic inequities (Kumashiro, 2024).

Examples of equity literacy practices include:

- **Examining curricular materials** for balanced representation and challenging stereotypes. This includes choosing texts and resources that do not merely add token diversity but authentically represent a wide array of identities and experiences by adding *diversity within diversity*.
- **Advocating for inclusive school policies** that consider the needs of all students and families, particularly those from marginalized communities. For

instance, questioning dress codes, attendance policies, or grading systems that might disproportionately impact certain student groups.
- **Reevaluating classroom norms** that may inadvertently privilege certain behaviors or ways of learning associated with White, middle-class cultural norms, like an overemphasis on a culturally-specific, assertive verbal participation style.

Equity literacy also involves understanding that implicit biases can shape teacher expectations and interpretations of student behavior. A teacher with equity literacy might reflect on whether their expectations for "appropriate" behavior are fair and inclusive or rooted in their own identity norms. For instance, rather than expecting all students to participate in the same way, teachers could explore diverse forms of engagement that validate different approaches to learning.

Coded Language

A critical aspect of racial and equity literacy is unlearning **coded language** – phrases that subtly reinforce stereotypes or biases by framing students in terms that signal unexamined assumptions. Terms like "high-achieving" or "at-risk" may initially seem neutral, but they can inadvertently signal racial or socioeconomic expectations that marginalize certain students. For example, "at-risk" is often used to label students based on socioeconomic status or racial identity rather than actual individual needs, which can limit opportunities for support and growth.

To disrupt the habit of *both thinking and speaking* in coded language, beginning teachers should:

- **Practice naming issues directly.** Instead of simply referring to "underperforming students," teachers can describe the systemic barriers in the developmental ecosystem that interact to impact academic performance, such as *lack of access to resources, inequitable school funding, or bias in assessments*.
- **Examine how language frames responsibility for educational outcomes.** For example, terms like "achievement gap" suggest that students are failing to meet a standard, while *"opportunity gap"* highlights systemic inequities that shape learning conditions (Howard, 2010). Shifting to systemic language helps teachers focus on addressing structural barriers rather than blaming students.
- **Describe behaviors or challenges in specific, nonjudgmental, observable terms rather than assigning vague labels.** Instead of describing a student as "challenging," teachers might focus on observable behaviors and the strategies that could support the student's success.
- **Encourage open discussion about inequities within the classroom.** By explicitly naming *race, class, and equity*, teachers can *developmentally*

model critical thinking and create space for students to engage in meaningful conversations about fairness and justice.

A teacher committed to avoiding coded thought and language might work actively to dismantle stereotypes by discussing issues like *resource disparities* or *racial identity* openly at school. This practice not only promotes transparency but also promotes a culture where others, particularly students, understand that their identities and experiences are acknowledged and respected.

By developing racial and equity literacy, beginning teachers can lay a strong foundation for antiracist teaching. These literacies enable educators to recognize and address systemic biases, understand the complex dynamics of race and privilege, and engage meaningfully with all students. Through direct language, honest self-reflection, and intentional practice, teachers create classrooms that are not only inclusive and equitable but also actively work to challenge and dismantle systemic inequities. In doing so, they model for students the importance of engaging with these issues directly, fostering a learning environment that values every student's identity and lived experience.

Applying Antiracist Developmental Frameworks in PK-12 Contexts

In PK-12 classrooms, teachers' interactions with students and the environments they create serve as powerful sites for either reinforcing or challenging systemic inequities. Classroom norms, disciplinary practices, curriculum content, and other daily routines are often packed with implicit cultural expectations rooted in dominant, historically White cultural norms. For educators aiming to dismantle these patterns, the classroom becomes a crucial space for critical reflection and intentional change. By applying antiracist frameworks to everyday activities, teachers not only address their own positionalities but also engage in practices that honor and support the identities of their students. This section provides practical approaches to integrating antiracist culturally responsive management, restorative practices, and critical examination of educational goals and curriculum content, all with the aim of fostering inclusive, equitable learning environments.

Antiracist "Culturally Responsive" Classroom Management

Culturally responsive classroom management (Milner, 2019) is a supportive environment that acknowledges and values students' identities and cultural backgrounds. *It is important to note that this type of cultural responsivity is race-visible and power and oppression-visible.* This approach goes beyond traditional classroom management techniques and superficial iterations of multicultural education (think "holidays and heroes") by recognizing that classroom norms are not neutral but often reflect the ways that *dominant cultural perspectives are asserted through systemic racism*, which can marginalize students who do not share these backgrounds. When teachers engage with antiracist culturally responsive principles, they actively work against these implicit biases, creating a classroom climate where all students feel seen and respected. This work is particularly crucial because classroom management strategies can either reinforce or disrupt systemic inequities. If teachers are not mindful, practices rooted in conformity and compliance can unintentionally perpetuate harm, especially for students from minoritized backgrounds.

Within the White Zone of Proximal Development (WZPD) framework, culturally responsive management means, in part, that teachers acknowledge their roles as mediators, intentionally facilitating a learning environment that actively challenges systemic racism. Strategies for creating an inclusive classroom environment include incorporating culturally relevant materials, celebrating diverse cultural traditions, holding high expectations for all learners, removing structural barriers, and establishing norms that respect all students' backgrounds (Gay, 2018; Winn, 2020). Because "celebrating diverse cultural traditions" has proven to be a slippery slope in the world of education for a lot of educators who are avoiding confronting racism, "cultural" educational buzzwords have been quick to devolve into surface-level, race-evasive, practices that do little, if anything, to actually promote equity, we will be clear to detail what this means (Gorski & Swalwell, 2015).

In this book, antiracist culturally responsive classroom management includes techniques that promote equity, such as using cooperative learning groups, integrating restorative practices, and incorporating student voice in classroom decision-making (Ladson-Billings, 1995; Winn, 2020; Yosso, 2005). Examples of these practices include:

- **Cooperative Learning Groups:** Assigning mixed-ability groups with both flexible and structured roles that frequently change, such as Project Based Learning, that allow students to meaningfully collaborate on projects, sharing responsibility and perspectives.
- **Restorative Practices:** Holding regular classroom circles where students can discuss conflicts, share personal updates, or set group goals helps build trust and a sense of community. Teachers can *model accountability by acknowledging their own mistakes and offering genuine apologies* when necessary, showing students that everyone in the classroom is a learner and responsible for maintaining a respectful environment (Morrison & Vaandering, 2012).
- **Promoting Student Voice and Critical Literacy:** Encouraging students to identify and discuss inequities they notice in the curriculum or biases in school policies provides an authentic space for critical literacy. Their insights and suggestions can shape classroom practices and learning materials, creating an

environment where students feel empowered to contribute to a more equitable and reflective classroom culture.

In various schools, the adoption of restorative justice circles has shown a significant reduction in suspensions and expulsions, fostering a more inclusive school climate where students feel their voices are heard and respected (González, 2012). Case studies showcasing effective culturally responsive management practices demonstrate how schools have successfully reduced disciplinary disparities and improved student engagement through these methods (Milner, 2019).

Restorative Practices

Restorative practices are a paradigm shift from behavior charts and zero-tolerance-style classroom management. As part of an antiracist educational context, restorative practices focus on repairing harm and restoring relationships rather than punitive measures. These practices aim to create a supportive school climate where students feel valued and respected (Winn, 2020). Within the WZPD framework, restorative practices help to recognize and dismantle systemic biases that contribute to conflict.

A step-by-step guide to implementing restorative justice circles include things like:

- Establishing community agreements
- Training staff and students
- Facilitating restorative "circles"
- Providing ongoing support and reflection

Examples of restorative practices reducing disciplinary disparities include schools where suspensions and expulsions have significantly decreased, and student-teacher relationships have improved (González, 2012).

Questioning Assumptions about What Education Is For

A critical examination of traditional educational goals reveals that many current practices may not align with antiracist principles. Traditional goals often emphasize standardized testing and individual achievement, which can perpetuate systemic inequities (Kendi, 2019). These goals can marginalize students from diverse backgrounds by valuing conformity and compliance over critical thinking and creativity.

Reimagining educational objectives involves promoting social justice, equity, and collective well-being. This includes *redefining success wherever possible within the institution to encompass civic engagement, critical thinking, and cultural perspective-taking* (Freire, 1970). Educators might actively question common practices such as having students walk in straight lines, sit in rows, and adhere strictly to bells signaling class changes. While these practices promote order, they can also reflect outdated notions of control and compliance that do not necessarily contribute to a positive learning environment. If tied to a punitive classroom management system, what could be arbitrary expectations could have serious long-term consequences for some students (consider "zero-tolerance policies"). Additionally, teachers should reflect on their own cultural assumptions about what constitutes a "good" student and what a "successful" education looks like. These assumptions are often based on teachers' positionalities and can influence how they perceive and interact with students (Milner, 2007; Utt & Tochluk, 2020).

When schools and educators redefine educational goals to support antiracist education, they demonstrate how shifting priorities can create more equitable and inclusive learning environments (Ladson-Billings, 2014). This shift is reflected in practices such as flexible seating, collaborative project-based learning, and inclusive decision-making processes that engage students, families, and communities (Yosso, 2005). These approaches recognize that education is not a fixed concept but can be shaped collectively, emphasizing the importance of community voices rather than leaving decisions solely to the school.

Making Opportunities for Developing Critical Literacy

Holiday observances in schools often reflect broader societal power structures, with school calendars typically privileging Christian and Western holidays. For this reason, they offer an everyday example of an opportunity for teachers to *guide students in developing critical literacy.*

School traditions can be so commonplace that they can feel almost "invisible" to those whose identities align with the dominant culture and for this reason, often go unchecked. The prioritization not only sidelines other cultural and religious traditions but also reinforces a hierarchy in which certain identities and histories are treated as the standard year after year. By examining these mundane practices critically, educators can help to disrupt these embedded biases and create more inclusive environments that respect the diversity of all students.

To extend this critical examination, teachers can guide students through norm-questioning activities, for instance, a critical literacy analysis of how holidays are represented in their school calendar. Teachers can guide students to take a closer look at which holidays are acknowledged and question whose stories are centered and whose are excluded. Beginning with a discussion on identity and representation, teachers can introduce holidays such as Christmas, Yom Kippur, Eid Ul-Fitr, Diwali, and Lunar New Year, exploring their significance and practices. Students then review their school's holiday calendar and research local demographics to assess whether these observances reflect the community's diversity, sparking conversations on equity and inclusion.

Facilitating group discussions where students brainstorm ways to make the school calendar more inclusive provides a practical application of their insights. However, these conversations can go beyond inclusion by encouraging students, depending on their developmental readiness, to reframe the concept of inclusion itself. Rather than simply adding "diverse holidays" to the existing calendar, students can critically examine how the dominant culture is centered in school traditions and imagine a truly multicultural calendar that equitably reflects the values and diversity of the United States. This extension deepens students' understanding of how even time structures and school practices can be vehicles for reinforcing or challenging societal norms, empowering them to advocate for a more representative school environment.

Now, let's explore practical examples that bring these concepts to life. In the following section, we will delve into a detailed comparison of two classroom environments. This comparison will illustrate the impact of what we will call *"traditional"* versus *"antiracist"* teaching practices in real-world educational settings.

Practical Example: A Tale of Two Classrooms

Mrs. Traditional's Classroom

When you step into Mrs. Traditional's 1st-grade classroom, you're greeted by a sense of order and predictability. Desks are arranged in uniform rows facing the front of the room, each one equipped with the same set of supplies. The walls are decorated with educational posters featuring prominent historical figures and scenes that feel reminiscent of textbooks – portraits of presidents, pioneers, and scientists. A large, colorful *behavior chart* by the whiteboard stands out. Every student's name is listed, and daily behavior is color-coded to indicate where each student "stands" in terms of following classroom expectations. It's a system that's easy to understand and, as Ms. Traditional might say, sets a clear standard for everyone.

On another wall, a *"Whole Body Listening"* poster outlines how to sit and focus, specifying "feet flat, hands in lap, eyes on the speaker." The library shelves are filled with classics, some dating back decades. Ms. Traditional curated this collection with her favorites from childhood and inherited books that filled her classroom when she first arrived. Some feature well-known figures like Martin Luther King Jr. and Cesar Chavez, read aloud during certain times of the year.

Seasonal decorations signal the coming of traditional holidays, like *Thanksgiving* and *Christmas*, which bring a warm, festive touch to the space. The overall feel is traditional and consistent, guided by Ms. Traditional's belief in discipline, respect, and providing a safe, consistent, loving place for her students, who may not have this at home. Her approach is also apparent in the emphasis on concepts like "grit" and "growth mindset," which are discussed at weekly assemblies as essential skills for academic and personal success. Ms. Traditional participates in professional development sessions and follows trauma-informed practices, and her takeaway has largely centered on thinking about how to support students in *overcoming challenges outside the classroom*. She maintains her view of the school as a stable, controlled environment where students can focus on learning (Duane & Winninghoff, 2023; Gorski, 2020).

Ms. WZPD's Classroom

Entering Ms. WZPD's 1st-grade classroom, the first thing you notice is the desk arrangement. Instead of rows, desks are clustered in small groups, encouraging *conversation and collaboration*. The walls are alive with color, featuring student artwork, cultural posters, and photographs that *reflect* the diversity of the *community and broader world*. Near the windows, a cozy reading corner is stocked with books that celebrate a wide range of experiences, cultures, and family structures. Titles are *carefully chosen* to reflect *"diversity within diversity,"* ensuring that multiple voices and perspectives are represented, from stories of everyday life to cultural folktales and historical accounts.

Instead of a traditional behavior chart, Ms. WZPD has designated a *"Restorative Practices"* corner, where students can take a break, talk through conflicts, or reflect with support. The space is inviting, with soft cushions, dim lighting, and posters encouraging students to share their feelings openly and work through challenges respectfully. In her classroom, behavior management focuses on *building community and accountability* rather than on public displays of compliance

Everywhere you look, elements of *Universal Design for Learning (UDL)* are integrated into the classroom setup (CAST, 2018). Visual aids, *multilingual materials*, and flexible learning tools are within reach, creating a space that adapts to different ways of engaging. *Communication with families* is another visible feature – flyers and announcements are available in multiple languages, and invitations to classroom events *encourage participation on families' terms*. It's clear that Ms. WZPD values these *partnerships,* framing them as an essential part of the learning process.

Mrs. WZPD's approach to teaching extends to *her own development*; her classroom reflects her commitment to deepening her racial and equity literacy. She attends professional development focused on antiracist practices and *racial literacy*, equipping her to create an environment where all students feel validated and respected. Her classroom is an active site of *inclusion,* shaped not only by her professional learning but also by her openness to student voices and experiences, which inform the space and the routines within it. Mrs. WZPD's setup and materials suggest an intentional effort to make each child feel they belong and are valued here, inviting them to *bring their full identities* into the learning experience.

Analysis of Classroom Environments

The Classroom Environment

Ms. Traditional's classroom setup, with its rows of desks and "Whole Body Listening" poster, reinforces a one-size-fits-all approach rooted in traditional expectations of compliance and focus. This physical arrangement reflects a teacher-centered model, where students are directed to follow routines and behavioral expectations established by the teacher. For students who thrive in more interactive or collaborative settings, this setup can be limiting, and the emphasis on traditional behavioral norms may inadvertently marginalize neurodivergent students or those who do not conform to these standards (Milner & Tenore, 2010; Milner, 2019).

In contrast, Ms. WZPD's classroom is arranged to prioritize student interaction and collaboration, with clusters of desks fostering a social learning environment. This aligns with contemporary educational theories that emphasize the importance of social interaction and cooperation. The presence of a "Restorative Practices" corner, instead of a public behavior chart, also signals a shift toward understanding behavior in a more developmental, inclusive way. Rather than focusing on compliance, Ms. WZPD encourages students to reflect on their actions and work through conflicts within a supportive framework. This approach promotes a classroom culture that values relationships and accountability, especially important in inclusive, culturally responsive settings.

Curriculum Choices and Representation

Ms. Traditional's classroom library, filled with books from her own childhood and older collections inherited from previous teachers, showcases a curriculum that reflects her personal experiences and the cultural norms of her formative years. Her selection of books and materials is limited to familiar, traditional perspectives, often focusing on "heroes and holidays" representations of diversity. This collection unintentionally reinforces a narrow view of cultural diversity, where students from non-dominant backgrounds may see themselves represented only in certain contexts or as "other." The limited scope of her library and reliance on holiday decorations further indicate a lack of awareness around deeper issues of representation and equity.

On the other hand, Ms. WZPD's classroom library and decor are curated with intentionality. By featuring books that provide "diversity within diversity," she ensures that students encounter a broad spectrum of identities and experiences beyond stereotypical or tokenistic portrayals (Adichie, 2009; Bishop, 1990). Her curriculum is guided by culturally sustaining pedagogy, which emphasizes honoring students' identities as part of their learning experience (Paris & Alim, 2017). Ms. WZPD's active commitment to racial literacy allows her to recognize the importance of these materials in shaping students' sense of belonging and engagement. Her classroom environment is not just inclusive but actively works to decenter Whiteness by presenting a variety of cultural perspectives and experiences as equally valuable.

Teacher Positionality and Racial Literacy

Ms. Traditional's choices reflect a positionality shaped by her own experiences in predominantly White, Eurocentric educational settings. Her approach to classroom management and curriculum lacks an explicit examination of how her background influences her decisions. For instance, her reliance on familiar books and historical figures from her own education and the adherence to school traditions around holidays suggest a limited awareness of how her identity affects her teaching. Concepts like "grit" and "growth mindset," presented in isolation, place the onus on students to overcome challenges individually without considering how systemic inequities might affect their learning experiences. This reflects a broader deficit perspective, where students' challenges are seen as obstacles to be overcome rather than issues to be addressed systemically. Mrs. Traditional's working assumption that her school is a safe place and not a site for potenital trauma should be interrogated (Duane & Winninghoff, 2023).

In contrast, Ms. WZPD demonstrates an ongoing commitment to deepening her racial literacy, understanding her positionality, and questioning her assumptions. She actively works to unlearn the biases embedded in her own socialization and incorporates antiracist practices to create a classroom environment that supports all students. By recognizing her own identity and the privileges associated with it, Ms. WZPD creates a learning space that not only values diversity but also seeks to confront and dismantle systemic inequities. Her intentional use of restorative practices and culturally sustaining materials reflects an awareness of her role in mediating learning in a way that is inclusive and empowering for her students (Yosso, 2005).

Classroom Management and Equity Literacy

Ms. Traditional's use of a behavior chart, prominently displayed with color-coded behavior indicators, aligns with her structured approach to classroom management. However, this strategy may unintentionally signal a lack of cultural responsiveness. The public nature of the chart can contribute to a classroom dynamic where students feel monitored and categorized, particularly those who may struggle with compliance due to differing cultural or neurodivergent needs. This management style reinforces conformity over individual expression, which can discourage students from engaging fully if they do not align with the behavioral norms of the classroom.

Ms. WZPD's choice to replace the behavior chart with a restorative practices corner signals a shift toward equity literacy in her approach to classroom management. By creating a space where students can reflect, she offers an alternative to traditional punitive measures, encouraging a more collaborative and reflective response to behavioral issues. This approach recognizes that traditional discipline practices often reflect biases embedded within educational institutions and seeks to reduce those biases by offering students a voice and choice in managing their behavior. The use of restorative practices fosters a sense of agency and accountability, allowing students to take an active role in their own social and emotional development.

Reflect and Practice Activities

Structured practice, such as working through case studies, critical questions, and guided activities, offers a controlled space for professionals to apply these antiracist frameworks and concepts. This approach enables individuals to test strategies, reflect on outcomes, and gain valuable insights without the pressures of real-time decision-making. Engaging in these exercises sharpens the ability to recognize biases, translate theory into practice, and implement antiracist principles effectively.

Case Study Analysis: Consequences of Exclusionary Discipline

As you read the fictional case study below, consider the complexities of short-term solutions and systemic change. After reading, you will use the Antiracist Praxis Model to analyze the situation and develop strategies for addressing the identified inequities.

Background

Marcus is a 13-year-old Black boy in the 7th grade who attends a middle school in a suburban neighborhood. Known for his quick wit and enthusiasm in class, Marcus is generally well-liked by his peers. However, he has been repeatedly sent out of class for minor disruptions, such as talking out of turn and not following directions immediately. These frequent disciplinary actions are causing him to miss significant instructional time, leading to a decline in his grades and increasing disengagement from school.

Marcus lives with his mother, Ms. Thompson, and two younger siblings. Ms. Thompson, a social worker, has recently become a single parent. She often works late evenings conducting home visits, which means there has been a change in the patterns of their household distribution of responsibilities and Marcus is now pitching in to take care of his siblings after school. Despite these responsibilities, Marcus manages to maintain a positive attitude, though he sometimes struggles to balance his home duties with his schoolwork.

Mr. Adams, Marcus's homeroom teacher, has a reputation for being strict but fair. He believes that consistency in enforcing rules is crucial for maintaining a disciplined environment. Over the past semester, Marcus has had in-school suspensions three times for minor infractions – twice for incomplete homework that resulted from the previous suspensions, as each suspension has resulted in him falling further behind in his coursework. After the third suspension, he was informed that this means that he can no longer attend the next field trip. He has begun to feel alienated from his peers and teachers. Mr. Adams has noticed Marcus's increasingly disengaged behavior and declining grades but feels compelled to follow the school's disciplinary policy.

Ms. Roberts, the school counselor, has been following Marcus's case with concern. She has tried to intervene by speaking with Marcus and his teachers, but her efforts have not led to significant changes. Ms. Roberts understands the changes Marcus is experiencing at home and is aware of the broader implications of exclusionary discipline practices, including the data on the negative developmental impacts for Black boys. However, she feels constrained by the school's policies and the prevailing attitudes among the teaching staff.

The school's principal, Mr. Hernandez, is a firm believer in maintaining high standards and discipline. He supports the teachers' decisions and believes that suspensions are necessary to ensure a safe and orderly learning environment. Despite being aware of the statistics showing that Black students are disproportionately affected by such practices, he has not implemented any alternative disciplinary approaches.

Marcus's frequent suspensions have led to him feeling increasingly isolated. He used to participate actively in class discussions and enjoy group projects, but now he often sits quietly and avoids eye contact with his teachers. His peers have noticed the change and some have started to distance themselves from him, fearing they might also get into trouble.

Analyze

To analyze the case study, use your understanding of the White Zones of Proximal Development and the Antiracist Praxis Model below to guide and organize your thinking about the complexities presented in this case study.

Step 1: Identify Inequities. Read the case study and identify specific inequities and their impacts. Note important background context, affected parties, key figures, root causes, and contributing factors.

Step 2: Perspective Exploration. Examine the perspectives of all involved, including students, families, teachers, and administrators. Reflect on how their backgrounds and experiences shape their views and how these perspectives influence the inequities.

Step 3: Ecological Analysis. Analyze broader contexts and processes affecting the situation. Consider class rules, school policies, teacher positionality, and societal values. Discuss how these layers interact within an ecological systems model.

Step 4: Identify Community Readiness. Research similar challenges in other schools. Reflect on past approaches and outcomes to assess potential change strategies and anticipate responses.

Step 5: Brainstorm Potential Actions. Generate short-term, actionable steps for immediate concerns and longer-term strategies for sustainable change. Focus on equity and antiracism.

Step 6: Identify Supportive Resources. Identify supportive resources, including mentors, organizations, educational materials, etc. Discuss how to leverage these resources effectively.

Step 7: Reflect on Potential Barriers. Consider potential barriers such as stakeholder resistance or logistical challenges. Analyze how these might impact implementation and discuss strategies for overcoming them.

Step 8: Develop Immediate and Long-Term Personal Action Steps. Outline a realistic plan with immediate and long-term actions. Ensure it aligns with identified resources and barriers.

Step 9: Reflect and Adapt. Reflect on the impact of your actions on the broader system. Analyze observations and outcomes, adjust strategies as needed, and incorporate feedback for continuous improvement.

Critical Questions

The reflection and discussion prompts below encourage your engagement with the chapter's content. In response, you can free-write rapid reactions, write longer papers supported by related literature, and/or formulate strategies through small group discussion in class.

1. How can teachers learn about *families and their strengths* to better support student success through an antiracist developmental lens? Walk through an example of how a teacher, while reflecting on their own positionality, might *plan for the first days of school* to build meaningful relationships with families, considering systemic factors and community influences that shape these interactions.
2. Explain how *teachers' positionality* impacts their classroom management and curriculum decisions. Why is understanding this important for antiracist practice?
3. What might a *classroom management plan* look like if it were designed to actively challenge systemic biases? Discuss key elements and practices involved.
4. Describe how teachers may use proxy approaches, such as 'multicultural' celebrations, to avoid directly addressing systemic racism and inequity. How can teachers develop the *racial and equity literacy* necessary to create educational experiences that meaningfully confront these issues?
5. Identify a popular educational concept or term that might *shift the responsibility of addressing systemic racism onto individual students* (e.g., "resilience"). Analyze its implications and propose how teachers can use language that *acknowledges systemic barriers* while also supporting student growth and development.

Interview: Exploring Antiracist Practices in Education

Assignment: Conduct an interview with an educator known for their commitment to antiracist practices in their classroom or school. Choose a teacher, administrator, or counselor engaged in antiracist work. Prepare questions focusing on their experiences, challenges, and development.

Sample Questions:

- What inspired you to incorporate antiracist practices in your teaching?
- What strategies or activities have been most effective in creating an antiracist classroom?
- What challenges have you faced, and how did you address them?
- How do you involve students and families in conversations about race and equity?
- How do you keep evolving your antiracist practices? What resources have been most valuable?

Analysis: Reflect on the responses and identify key themes. Compare insights with concepts like the WZPD framework, culturally responsive teaching, and racial literacy.

Chapter Summary

- The "savior" narrative in teaching points to interpersonal and individual perspectives; teachers need to understand their role within a larger ecological system
- Developing a reflective practice can help teachers build critical consciousness by identifying biases, analyzing their positionality, and understanding how systemic factors impact their teaching practices and their roles as mediators of learning with a capacity to either reinforce or dismantle systemic inequities.
- Integrating restorative practices shifts classroom management from punitive measures to approaches that repair harm, build community, and foster accountability.
- Developing racial and equity literacy equips teachers to challenge coded language and race-evasive practices disguised as "culture," deepening their engagement with antiracist pedagogy.

Recommended Resources

The following books, articles, and other resources may help you deepen your understanding of antiracism in PK-12 educational contexts.

- Derman-Sparks, L., & Edwards, J. O (2020). *Anti-bias education for young children and ourselves*. 2nd Edition. NAEYC.

- Helms, J. E. (2020). *A race is a nice thing to have: A guide to being a White person or understanding the White persons in your life* (3rd ed.). Cognella.
- Embrace Race https://www.embracerace.org/
- Learning for Justice. https://www.learningforjustice.org/
- Matias, C. E., & Gorski, P. (Eds.). (2023). *The Other Elephant in the (class) room: White Liberalism and the Persistence of Racism in Education.* Teachers College Press.
- Reconceptualizing Early Childhood Education (RECE). https://receinternational.org/
- Rethinking Schools. https://rethinkingschools.org/
- Teaching While White. https://www.teachingwhilewhite.org/podcast

References

Adichie, C. N. (2009). *The danger of a single story.* TEDGlobal. https://www.ted.com/talks/chimamanda_ngozi_adichie_the_danger_of_a_single_story

Ahmad, F. Z., & Boser, U. (2014). America's leaky pipeline for teachers of color: Getting more teachers of color into the classroom. *Center for American Progress.*

Beauchamp, C., & Thomas, L. (2009). Understanding teacher identity: An overview of issues in the literature and implications for teacher education. *Cambridge Journal of Education, 39*(2), 175–189.

Banes, L. C., Ambrose, R. C., Bayley, R., Restani, R. M., & Martin, H. A. (2018). Mathematical classroom discussion as an equitable practice: Effects on elementary English learners' performance. *Journal of Language, Identity & Education, 17*(6), 416–433.

Bishop, R. S. (1990). Mirrors, windows, and sliding glass doors. *Perspectives: Choosing and Using Books for the Classroom, 6*(3), ix–xi.

Black, P., & Wiliam, D. (1998). Assessment and classroom learning. *Assessment in Education: Principles, Policy & Practice, 5*(1), 7–74.

Bonilla-Silva, E. (2021). *Racism without racists: Color-blind racism and the persistence of racial inequality in America.* Rowman & Littlefield.

Bonilla-Silva, E., & Embrick, D. G. (2008). Recognizing the likelihood of reproducing racism. *Everyday Antiracism: Getting Real about Race in School,* 334–336.

CAST. (2018). *Universal Design for Learning guidelines version 2.2.* https://udlguidelines.cast.org

Derman-Sparks, L., & Edwards, J. O. (2020). *Anti-bias education for young children and ourselves* (2nd ed.). National Association for the Education of Young Children.

Duane, A., & Winninghoff, A. (2023). The road ahead: Moving beyond ACEs in transformative SEL. *Social and Emotional Learning: Research, Practice, and Policy, 1*(2023), 100002.

Freire, P. (1970). *Pedagogy of the oppressed.* Continuum.

García, O., & Kleifgen, J. A. (2020). Translanguaging and literacies. *Reading research quarterly, 55*(4), 553–571.

García, O., Johnson, S. I., Seltzer, K., & Valdés, G. (2017). *The translanguaging classroom: Leveraging student bilingualism for learning* (pp. v–xix). Philadelphia, PA: Caslon.

Gay, G. (2018). *Culturally responsive teaching: Theory, research, and practice* (3rd ed.). Teachers College Press.

Goldin, S., Duane, A., & Khasnabis, D. (2021, December). Interrupting the weaponization of trauma-informed practice: "... who were you really doing the 'saving'for?". In *The educational forum* (Vol. 86, No. 1, pp. 5–25). Routledge.

González, T. (2012). Keeping kids in schools: Restorative justice, punitive discipline, and the school to prison pipeline. *Journal of Law & Education, 41*(2), 281–335.

Gorski, P. (2020). How trauma-informed are we, really? *ASCD*. https://www.ascd.org/el/articles/how-trauma-informed-are-we-really

Gorski, P. C., & Swalwell, K. (2015). Equity literacy for all. *Educational Leadership, 72*(6), 34–40.

Fray, L., & Gore, J. (2018). Why people choose teaching: A scoping review of empirical studies, 2007–2016. *Teaching and Teacher Education, 75*, 153–163.

Helms, J. E. (2020). *A race is a nice thing to have: A guide to being a White person or understanding the White persons in your life* (3rd ed.). Cognella.

Herrera, A. (2021). *Compounded Whiteness: White teacher antiracist ideological commitment development in predominantly white elementary schools*. University of California, Davis.

Howard, T. C. (2010). *Why race and culture matter in schools: Closing the opportunity gap in America's classrooms*. Teachers College Press.

Ireland, J. D. (Trans.). (1997). *The Udana: Inspired utterances of the Buddha* (Tittha Sutta, Ud. 6.4). Kandy, Sri Lanka: Buddhist Publication Society. Available at Access to Insight.

Iruka, I. U., Gardner-Neblett, N., Telfer, N. A., Ibekwe-Okafor, N., Curenton, S. M., Sims, J., ... & Neblett, E. W. (2022). Effects of racism on child development: Advancing antiracist developmental science. *Annual Review of Developmental Psychology, 4*(1), 109–132.

Johnson, D. W., Johnson, R. T., & Holubec, E. J. (1998). *Cooperation in the classroom*. Allyn and Bacon.

Turner, B. (2019). Teaching kindness isn't enough. *Learning for Justice, 63*(Fall), 41–43. https://www.learningforjustice.org/magazine/fall-2019/teaching-kindness-isnt-enough

Kelty, N. E., & Wakabayashi, T. (2020). Family engagement in schools: Parent, educator, and community perspectives. *Sage Open, 10*(4), 2158244020973024.

Kendi, I. X. (2019). *How to be an antiracist*. One World.

Kishimoto, K. (2018). Anti-racist pedagogy: From faculty's self-reflection to organizing within and beyond the classroom. *Race Ethnicity and Education, 21*(4), 540–554.

Kumashiro, K. K. (2024). *Against Common Sense: Teaching and Learning Toward Social Justice*. Taylor & Francis.

Ladson-Billings, G. (1995). Toward a theory of culturally relevant pedagogy. *American Educational Research Journal, 32*(3), 465–491. https://doi.org/10.3102/00028312032003465

Ladson-Billings, G. (2014). Culturally relevant pedagogy 2.0: a.k.a. the remix. *Harvard Educational Review, 84*(1), 74–84.

Leonardo, Z., & Manning, L. (2017). White historical activity theory: Toward a critical understanding of white zones of proximal development. *Race Ethnicity and Education, 20*(1), 15–29.

Love, B. L. (2019). *We want to do more than survive: Abolitionist teaching and the pursuit of educational freedom*. Beacon Press.

Matthews, A. (2021). Reversing the gaze on race, social justice, and inclusion in public librarianship. *Education for Information, 37*(2), 187–202.

Milner IV, H. R. (2007). Race, culture, and researcher positionality: Working through dangers seen, unseen, and unforeseen. *Educational Researcher, 36*(7), 388–400.

Milner, H. R. (2010). *Start where you are, but don't stay there: Understanding diversity, opportunity gaps, and teaching in today's classrooms*. Harvard Education Press.

Milner, H. R., & Tenore, F. B. (2010). Classroom management in diverse classrooms. *Urban Education, 45*(5), 560–603. https://doi.org/10.1177/0042085910377290

Milner, H. R. (2019). Culturally responsive classroom management. (pp. 1–20). *Oxford Research Encyclopedia of Education*. https://doi.org/10.1093/acrefore/9780190264093.013.782

Morrison, B. E., & Vaandering, D. (2012). Restorative justice: Pedagogy, praxis, and discipline. *Journal of School Violence, 11*(2), 138–155. https://doi.org/10.1080/15388220.2011.653322

Olsen, B. (2015). *Teaching what they learn, learning what they live: How teachers' personal histories shape their professional development*. Routledge.

Paris, D., & Alim, H. S. (2017). *Culturally sustaining pedagogies: Teaching and learning for justice in a changing world*. Teachers College Press.

Reyes, G., & Aronson, B. (2022). "It reeks of first-wave whiteness": A reimagined critical whiteness studies and feminist of color teacher education. *International Journal of Qualitative Studies in Education, 35*(7), 737–743.

Rogoff, B. (2003). *The cultural nature of human development*. (pp. 340–361). Oxford university press.

Sarma, V. R. (2000). The story of the blind men and the elephant in Indian tradition: A comparative approach. *International Journal of Hindu Studies, 4*(2), 163–172.

Suzuki, S., Johnson, S. K., & Ferreira van Leer, K. (2023). Situating critical consciousness within the developmental system: Insights from the Phenomenological Variant of Ecological Systems Theory. In L. Rapa & E. Godfrey (Eds.), *Critical consciousness: Expanding theory and measurement*. (pp. 41–62). Cambridge University Press.

Syed, M., Santos, C., Yoo, H. C., & Juang, L. P. (2018). Invisibility of racial/ethnic minorities in developmental science: Implications for research and institutional practices. *American Psychologist, 73*(6), 812.

Tomlinson, C. A. (2014). *The differentiated classroom: Responding to the needs of all learners* (2nd ed.). ASCD.

Tomlinson, C. A. (2017). *How to differentiate instruction in academically diverse classrooms* (3rd ed.). ASCD.

Umasvati. (Trans. with commentary). (1994). *Tattvartha Sutra: That which is* (N. Tatia, Trans.). HarperCollins.

Utt, J., & Tochluk, S. (2020). White teacher, know thyself: Improving anti-racist praxis through racial identity development. *Urban Education, 55*(1), 125–152.

Vygotsky, L. S. (1978). *Mind in society: The development of higher psychological processes*. Harvard University Press.

Winn, M. T. (2020). *Justice on both sides: Transforming education through restorative justice*. (pp. 7–19). Harvard Education Press.

Wood, D., Bruner, J. S., & Ross, G. (1976). The role of tutoring in problem-solving. *Journal of Child Psychology and Psychiatry, 17*(2), 89–100.

Wood, J. L., Harris, F., & Qas, M. K. A. S. (2020). *The capitol of school suspensions II: Examining the racial exclusion of black students in sacramento city unified school district*. Community College Equity Assessment Lab.

Yosso, T. J. (2005). Whose culture has capital? A critical race theory discussion of community cultural wealth. *Race Ethnicity and Education, 8*(1), 69–91.

Chapter 4

An Antiracist Developmental View of Higher Education

Introduction

First, let's try something. Picture a college student. Who comes to mind? Perhaps a young adult, right out of high school, taking a full courseload without the constraints of full-time work or caregiving. If you did, you would not be alone. This image of the "traditional" college student is so ingrained that it still shapes many of the guiding systems and policies of higher education. But the reality is far more complex and today's students are far more intersectionally diverse.

Across the United States, the majority of students are now what scholars call *"post-traditional."* These students defy the outdated "traditional" mold; they are older, they work, they are parents, and they come from a wide array of racial and socioeconomic backgrounds. Yet, despite this diversity, higher education institutions continue to center their practices around a much more homogeneous, privileged student archetype (Navarette, 2021). This misalignment not only marginalizes post-traditional students but also upholds systemic barriers that disproportionately affect students of color, compounding the challenges they face as they strive for academic success (Iloh, 2018; Navarette, 2021).

Consider that nearly 85% of college students today could be described as post-traditional in one way or another, with significant representation from racially minoritized backgrounds (Navarette, 2021; Shumaker & Wood, 2016). And while higher education policies often remain tied to "traditional" norms, the need for antiracist, developmentally-informed strategies has never been greater. The persistence of *inequitable practices*, such as *rigid class schedules, limited support for working students, and racially exclusive campus cultures*, underscores the urgency for change (Glowacki-Dudka, 2019; Kuh, 2008).

University settings **function as complex ecosystems**, akin to small cities, intricately woven into the broader communities where they are located. These institutions not only interact with their immediate surroundings but also embody nested layers of influence, from local dynamics to national and global contexts. Understanding higher education through an bioecological lens allows us to make visible the various layers and interactions between these contexts, providing a clearer picture of how universities operate and affect those within them.

In terms of racial justice, higher education institutions are not isolated entities; they are embedded in sociohistorical and cultural frameworks that reflect and shape broader societal values. These institutions can either sustain and reinforce systemic racism or serve as pivotal spaces for challenging and disrupting inequitable practices. Ideally, early career professionals bring a foundational understanding of how intersecting systems influence student identity development and educational outcomes to their work at universities. Higher education can be envisioned as a place for wholeness, social justice, and liberation (Rendón & Cantú, 2009).

This chapter is for anyone aiming to understand higher education as a context for fostering student identity development through an antiracist developmental framework. Many child and adolescent development majors find employment in higher education, whether in student affairs, academic advising, administration, or faculty roles. This chapter bridges the fields of developmental psychology, antiracist practice, and higher education strategies to equip pre- and early-career professionals with the tools to both navigate and disrupt these spaces.

This chapter's key features include:

- An Introduction to the Multicontextual Model for Diverse Learning Environments (MMDLE)
- Affirming and Sustaining Student Identity
- Aligning Professional Practices with Antiracist Principles
- Critical Issues and Considerations
- Reflect and Practice Activities
- Recommended Resources

An Ecological Model for Higher Education

You've been introduced to several developmental frameworks in this book that are critical extensions of, or can be understood through, Bronfenbrenner's bioecological model. We hope that you are beginning to feel some familiarity and ease moving through these kinds of models. This chapter introduces another ecological model specifically designed for understanding the racial climate of diverse university settings: the **Multicontextual Model for Diverse Learning Environments** (Hurtado et al., 2012). The MMDLE adapts and extends Bronfenbrenner's foundational concept, positioning student identities and their dynamic interactions at the core of multiple, interconnected contexts within higher education.

Bronfenbrenner's bioecological model (Bronfenbrenner & Morris, 2006) provides a framework that conceptualizes human development as influenced by various layers of environment, from the immediate settings of the microsystem to the broader cultural and policy-driven macrosystem. His model underscores the importance of understanding development as a multifaceted process shaped by interactions within and across these levels. In the context of higher education, this ecological approach offers a valuable lens for analyzing how diverse elements – ranging from peer relationships to institutional policies – interact to shape student outcomes.

The MMDLE builds upon Bronfenbrenner's concept by emphasizing the *racial and cultural dynamics* embedded within these systems. It provides a comprehensive organization of how students' identities, and experiences are shaped not only by their immediate interactions but also by broader institutional and sociohistorical forces (Hurtado et al., 2012). This approach *bridges critical bioecological theory with the features of higher education*, where diversity, inclusion, and equity play central roles in student development.

From Bronfenbrenner to the MMDLE: Bridging Understanding

Before diving into the critical extension of the MMDLE, it is helpful to briefly review and have Bronfenbrenner's foundational bioecological model at hand. This model, often depicted as a series of nested circles, places the individual at the center, surrounded by various environmental systems that interact to influence development. Each system in the model is meant to represent the multiple interactions occurring in the lives of individuals:

Microsystem: The immediate environment where *direct* interactions take place, such as relationships with peers, teachers, and family members.
Mesosystem: The *connections* between different microsystems, such as how family life interacts with school experiences.
Exosystem: External influences that do not involve the individual directly but still have an *indirect* impact, such as a parent's workplace or school board policies.
Macrosystem: The broader cultural and societal norms, values, and political influences that *shape the environment*.
Chronosystem: The dimension of *time*, considering life transitions and sociohistorical events that affect the individual over time (Bronfenbrenner & Morris, 2006).

This ecological model highlights that development is not static; it is influenced by multiple interacting layers that dynamically shape individual experiences. Understanding these foundational systems provides a **scaffold** for exploring how higher education can be analyzed using a *similar*, yet more *contextually specific*, approach.

The **Multicontextual Model for Diverse Learning Environments** then adapts the levels of the bioecological system by positioning them within a framework that accounts for *racial and cultural dynamics in higher education*. According to Hurtado et al. (2012), higher education institutions function as ecosystems where policies, cultural norms, and student demographics interact to create complex learning environments. The MMDLE not only incorporates the structures described by Bronfenbrenner but also integrates concepts from critical race theory, emphasizing how power dynamics and systemic racism influence student experiences and outcomes. *The authors recommend reviewing Hurtado et al. (2012) to explore the visual representation of the MMDLE model, as this chapter focuses solely on the theoretical components. The figure can be accessed through the citations and links provided in the Recommended Resources and References sections at the end of this chapter.*

Components of the MMDLE Explained

Understanding the MMDLE involves examining each of its components to grasp how **interconnected contexts** within higher education influence student experiences. The following sections break down the model's key elements, highlighting their roles in shaping inclusive and supportive educational environments.

Sociohistorical Context: The MMDLE situates the institution within a sociohistorical backdrop that encompasses larger societal forces, such as civil rights movements, demographic shifts, and legislative actions related to education (Hurtado et al., 2012). This layer highlights that universities do not operate in isolation; they are influenced by external pressures and public discourse, which shape institutional policies and practices.

Institutional Context: Corresponding to Bronfenbrenner's **mesosystem**, the institutional context in the MMDLE includes the policies, practices, and structures that define the educational environment. This encompasses aspects such as admissions policies, diversity initiatives, faculty representation, and support services that contribute to the overall climate of the university. Research has shown that a supportive institutional context correlates with improved educational outcomes for racially diverse student populations (Hurtado et al., 2012).

Campus Climate and Organizational Practices: The MMDLE adds a layer that Bronfenbrenner's theory does not explicitly address: the *behavioral and organizational dimensions of campus life*. These dimensions involve the attitudes, norms, and behaviors exhibited by students, faculty, and administrators, which collectively contribute to an institution's culture. Campus climate plays a pivotal role in determining whether students feel welcomed, supported, and motivated to engage (Hurtado et al., 2012). This climate, shaped by both structural and interpersonal elements, can either reinforce systemic inequities or serve as a space for progressive change.

Microsystem and Student Interactions: At the individual level, the MMDLE emphasizes the direct relationships and interactions students have with their peers, instructors, and campus staff. These relationships influence how students perceive their place within the university and affect their academic and personal growth. A positive **microsystem** fosters a sense of belonging and psychological safety, essential for the development of racially minoritized students (Hurtado et al., 2012).

Multilayered Outcomes: The MMDLE ultimately points to student outcomes as products of interactions across these diverse contexts. Outcomes include *academic achievement, social development, and identity formation*, all of which are impacted by the quality of the educational environment (Hurtado et al., 2012). This model encourages institutions to *assess* how well they support students from various backgrounds and to recognize that equitable educational experiences require systemic, intentional efforts at all levels of interaction.

Applying the MMDLE

Understanding and applying the MMDLE as a lens to view the complex interactions between systems in higher education and the larger cultural context can help guide institutions in creating environments that not only reflect compositional diversity but also promote inclusive and supportive climates. Hurtado et al. (2012) argue that true diversity is multifaceted and requires an *alignment of structural diversity, campus climate, and educational practices that facilitate positive intergroup interactions*. The MMDLE provides a roadmap for assessing how policies and practices align with these goals and highlights areas where institutions can improve to better serve racially diverse populations.

The MMDLE's comprehensive modeling emphasizes that *changes in policy or practice at one level could influence other areas of the educational ecosystem*. For instance, enhancing faculty diversity not only interacts with the institutional context but also interacts with the microsystem by providing role models for students. Similarly, policies promoting inclusive curricula contribute to a more affirming campus climate, reinforcing students' sense of identity and belonging. This model serves as a potentially powerful tool for early career professionals in higher education who would like structure around making visible and recognizing that student experiences are embedded within broader, complex systems of power and privilege and then being able to see where their work fits into this picture.

To *illustrate the application of the MMDLE*, consider a university initiative designed to increase retention and graduation rates among racially minoritized students. This effort begins by recognizing the institution's **sociohistorical context**, including past challenges related to racial diversity and responses to student activism that demanded more inclusive practices. The university's approach takes into account significant social justice movements that have influenced its policies over time. Within the **institutional context**, new policies are introduced, such as holistic admissions processes and targeted faculty recruitment to enhance diversity. Programs like mentorship networks and specialized financial aid for underrepresented students are also established. To address *campus climate and organizational practices*, surveys and focus groups are conducted, revealing areas of support as well as persistent issues like microaggressions. Positive findings include peer-led student organizations that provide community, while areas of concern lead to the development of outside and faculty or staff-led learning communities around antiracism for faculty and staff. At the **microsystem context**, the initiative forms student learning communities that connect students with peer mentors and faculty advisors sharing similar backgrounds or interests, nurturing belonging. Finally, the *outcomes* of these efforts are assessed through both academic performance metrics and qualitative measures, such as student engagement and identity development. These insights help the university refine its strategies, ensuring that programs align with antiracist principles and contribute to systemic change in higher education.

Affirming and Sustaining Student Identity in Higher Education

Identity plays a crucial role in how students perceive themselves and engage within educational spaces. When institutions affirm students' racial, ethnic, and cultural backgrounds, it fosters validation of their lived experiences, contributing to a sense of belonging and increased academic self-efficacy. Research has demonstrated that this validation is particularly significant for Latine students, who *often face a disconnect between their identities and institutional practices*. As noted by Gulley (2021), labeling students as "nontraditional" perpetuates feelings of being outsiders, resulting in psychological distress and self-doubt (Navarette, 2021). The research brief by Ferreira van Leer et al. (2024) underscores the importance of cultural representation within higher education and the role it plays in student success, particularly in Hispanic-Serving Institutions (HSIs).

Practical Strategies for Identity Affirmation

To create educational spaces that affirm student identities, institutions can:

- Prioritize hiring faculty who represent the diverse identities of the student body. This has been shown to improve student outcomes and contribute to a more inclusive curriculum that includes a range of perspectives and experiences (Ferreira van Leer et al., 2024).
- Foster curriculum development that embeds cultural knowledge and perspectives across various disciplines – not just within those dedicated to this endeavor, such as Ethnic Studies. As Ferreira van Leer et al. (2024) indicate, students express a desire for their culture to be reflected in course topics, readings, and activities beyond isolated instances.

- Implement structured academic and non-academic supports that cater to the unique needs of adult learners balancing work, family responsibilities, and their education (Navarette, 2021).

Aligning with Antiracist Principles

Institutions must move beyond token gestures of diversity to practices that challenge deficit narratives and create an environment where students know themselves to be genuinely included and valued. The gap between student demographics and faculty representation has an impact: many students feel that their identities are inadequately represented, which impacts their sense of belonging and engagement (Ferreira van Leer et al., 2024).

Shifting Institutional Perspectives

Colleges often remain out of sync with the needs of racially marginalized students, and to improve retention, colleges must acknowledge that students who feel connected to their educational journey are more likely to succeed (Navarette, 2021). Implementing high-impact educational practices that are inclusive and widely accessible – not just limited to learning communities or special projects – can help bridge this gap.

Recommendations for Higher Education

For higher education institutions to foster inclusivity, they can:

- Embed identity representation into faculty hiring, curriculum, and student support services to reflect and validate the diverse identities within the student population.
- Enhance awareness and visibility of institutional designations like HSIs to strengthen the organizational identity as one that is committed to serving Latine students, as advocated by Garcia et al. (2019) and Ferreira van Leer et al. (2024).

Integrating these strategies into the framework of higher education typically aligns with antiracist practices by challenging systemic inequities and fostering a holistic, supportive learning environment for a broad range of student identities.

Intersectionality and Critical Consciousness in Student Development

Integrating intersectionality into student development initiatives and education helps higher education institutions foster a comprehensive understanding for all of how intersecting social identities – such as race, gender, socioeconomic status, and sexuality – shape student experiences (Hurtado et al., 2012). The term **intersectionality**, introduced by Crenshaw (1989, 1991), highlights that individuals do not experience their identities in isolation but through *interwoven systems of privilege and oppression*. Recognizing these dynamics is key to addressing the unique challenges and opportunities that students encounter in their educational journeys.

Equally important is the development of **critical consciousness**, a process through which individuals learn to perceive and challenge social, political, and economic contradictions (Freire, 1970). In the context of higher education, fostering critical consciousness involves guiding students to recognize how their identities intersect with systemic structures that influence their lives. This heightened awareness empowers students to question societal norms, engage in dialogue about equity and justice, and become active participants in creating a more inclusive campus culture (Gurin, et al., 2002; Suzuki et al., 2023).

By embedding both intersectional thinking and critical consciousness into student development programs, higher education institutions promote deeper cognitive, emotional, and social growth. These approaches validate students' identities, encourage resilience, and equip them with the tools needed to advocate for change, supporting a campus climate that embraces diversity and promotes equity (Hurtado et al., 2012).

Supporting Programs and Initiatives

To integrate intersectional thinking and critical consciousness into the student experience, higher education professionals can support targeted programs that enable students to explore, reflect upon, and act on issues related to their own identities. Some examples include the following:

- **Identity Development Workshops and Dialogues** Workshops centered on social identity development create structured opportunities for students *to explore their own identities within the context of systemic power structures*. For instance, sessions that address intersecting identities – such as those around race, gender, socioeconomic background, and sexuality – encourage students to examine how these identities inform their lived experiences. These workshops are most impactful when they incorporate critical reflection, discussions, and peer engagement, allowing students to connect personal insights with broader societal issues (Gurin et al., 2002; Hurtado et al., 2012; Suzuki et al., 2023).
- **Leadership Programs with a Social Justice Lens** Leadership programs aimed at cultivating social justice awareness can help students develop a sense of agency in addressing equity-related issues on campus and beyond. By incorporating principles of intersectionality and critical consciousness, these programs empower students to critically analyze their positionality and the

power dynamics within their social contexts. Research shows that such experiences *deepen students' understanding of civic responsibility,* preparing them to become advocates for change in diverse communities (Gonzalez et al., 2020).
- **Collaborative Reflection and Peer-Led Activities** Engaging students in reflective, peer-led discussions fosters an inclusive environment where diverse experiences and perspectives are valued. Activities such as *intergroup dialogues*, storytelling sessions, and *affinity group discussions* help students process their individual experiences and appreciate others' viewpoints. These interactions, facilitated by well-trained peers or faculty, are particularly effective in reinforcing a sense of community and shared commitment to equity and justice (Rendón, 2006). They also promote empathy, build community bonds, and *empower students to co-create* a supportive and inclusive campus climate.

Antiracism and Development

Incorporating intersectional and critical consciousness approaches into student development programs can enrich educational environments and contribute to students' cognitive, social, and emotional growth. These practices do more than influence academic outcomes; they help students build skills such as resilience in the face of systemic oppression, social responsibility, and a commitment to social justice:

- **Enhancing Critical Thinking and Problem-Solving** Programs that integrate intersectionality and critical consciousness encourage students to analyze social structures and their roles within them. This type of engagement helps students think critically and strengthens their analytical skills, allowing them to approach complex social issues with an informed, multifaceted perspective. Research shows that exposure to diverse perspectives and structured interactions can enhance cognitive development, especially in areas like problem-solving and moral reasoning (Gonzalez et al., 2020; Gurin et al., 2002; Hurtado et al., 2012).
- **Building Empathy and Relational Skills** Programs centered on intersectionality and social justice can foster empathy and improve relational skills by encouraging students to connect with peers from different backgrounds. Structured opportunities for dialogue and collaboration help students develop active listening skills and deepen their understanding of various experiences. These skills are valuable in the classroom and essential in professional settings (Gonzalez et al., 2020; Rendón, 2006). Supporting students in this way contributes to more inclusive and collaborative campus communities.
- **Promoting Community Resilience and a Sense of Agency** Engagement in activities that enhance critical consciousness helps students develop a stronger sense of agency and purpose. Recognizing systemic barriers and learning how to respond collectively shifts the focus from individual coping

strategies to a broader, community-based approach (Navarette, 2021). Resilience, in this context, becomes a shared strength supported by community solidarity and collective action. This approach challenges deficit-based perspectives and reinforces the idea that students are not alone in their experiences (Gonzalez et al., 2020).

- **Addressing Imposter Syndrome and Bias** Imposter syndrome, especially among students from marginalized backgrounds, can undermine self-confidence and hinder a sense of belonging. Framing imposter syndrome as a *response to systemic bias* rather than an individual shortcoming can be transformative (Ogunyemi et al., 2020). Programs that help students identify external factors contributing to imposter syndrome empower them to reframe what they may have previously been experiencing as an individual shortcoming within a larger systemic framework, for instance, systemic racism (Navarette, 2021). Explicitly noting experiences, such as those of *institutional racelighting,* can help to strengthen a sense of self-worth (Crenshaw, 1991; Wood & Harris, 2024). This support can improve students' academic engagement and persistence.
- **Encouraging Lifelong Learning and Leadership** Engagement with social justice and critical consciousness initiatives prepares students to extend these values beyond the classroom into their future careers and leadership roles. Research indicates that students exposed to these practices are more likely to contribute to community development and act as agents of change (Freire, 1970; Gurin et al., 2002). This emphasis on lifelong learning benefits students individually and reinforces the institution's role in developing informed, active participants in society.

By fostering these developmental outcomes, higher education institutions create academic environments where students are prepared to excel academically and are motivated to enact meaningful change. Integrating intersectionality and critical consciousness into educational practices ensures alignment with values of equity, justice, and continuous personal and collective growth.

Centering Relationships and Emotional Support

The Role of Relationships in Development Strong, supportive relationships are foundational for fostering trust, motivation, and overall well-being. Developmental psychology emphasizes the importance of secure relationships in promoting positive outcomes, especially for students who may face systemic barriers.

Implementing Supportive Structures To center relationships and emotional support, higher education professionals should:

- Create mentorship programs that connect students with faculty or peers who share or understand their backgrounds and experiences.

- Develop peer support groups that allow students to share their stories, navigate challenges collectively, and build a sense of community.
- Provide counseling and support services that are culturally responsive and trauma-informed, recognizing the emotional toll of systemic discrimination.

Antiracist Principles in Practice Centering relationships aligns with antiracist efforts by ensuring that support systems address the full range of student needs, acknowledging their experiences of marginalization and working to counteract them through intentional, supportive practices.

Engaging in Advocacy

Advocacy is not just an act of social change but a critical component of student development. Participating in advocacy activities allows students to develop leadership skills, agency, and a deeper understanding of societal structures. Developmental theory supports the idea that when students are empowered to engage in change, they build confidence and a sense of purpose.

Strategies for Professionals

Early-career professionals can:

- Support and mentor students in organizing and leading advocacy initiatives.
- Advocate for policy changes that benefit racially minoritized students, such as revising bias response protocols and promoting inclusive hiring practices.
- Facilitate workshops and panels that discuss the intersections of policy, practice, and social justice, encouraging students to reflect on their roles as future leaders.

Engaging students in advocacy enhances their development by promoting active learning and fostering a sense of belonging within their communities. It encourages them to see themselves as capable agents of change, contributing to their long-term academic and personal growth.

Developmentally Informed Mentorship and Support Systems

Mentorship plays a pivotal role in the development of students, particularly those from racially minoritized backgrounds who face systemic racism and structural barriers in higher education. While pairing students with mentors of similar backgrounds is often the first strategy implemented, it is essential to approach this thoughtfully.

Representation as a Place to Start

Although *extensive* research supports race representation in mentorship for fostering positive identity development, choosing representation as a primary or sole approach can also become an excuse for institutions, particularly White faculty and staff, to avoid necessary growth and engagement across identity lines. Limiting thinking to a 'like-with-like' approach risks placing an undue burden on faculty and staff of color, often expecting them to shoulder the mentorship of most racially diverse students, which contributes to inequitable distribution of workload, referred to as *emotional labor* and the *diversity tax*. Furthermore, there is significant diversity within identity groups, and shared racial or cultural backgrounds do not automatically mean shared experiences or perspectives. Recognizing these nuances and complexities encourages mentorship practices that are inclusive, thoughtful, and balanced in a way that benefits all students and pushes mentors to grow. Institutions must carefully consider the complexity of mentorship dynamics and avoid one-size-fits-all approaches to support student development.

Reflective Practice for Mentors

Mentors should engage in **ongoing reflective practices** to understand their biases, positionality, and the power dynamics present in their relationships with students. This involves mentors asking themselves questions such as: "Am I projecting my experiences onto my mentee?" or "Am I adequately recognizing the unique experiences my mentee brings to this relationship?" An example of reflective practice could be a mentor reviewing their interactions and considering how they might have unconsciously reinforced power imbalances. For White mentors, understanding how their racial privilege might influence their guidance is crucial. Taking time to better understand intersecting identities, such as class, religion, and race can help mentors to realize the power they hold in the university context. Seeing student strengths, for instance, shifting from deficit-based to asset-based framing is vital. Mentors should be guided in ways to explore and identify the strengths a student of color has developed through their experiences, rather than assuming or emphasizing perceived gaps.

Navigating and Resisting a Racist System

A critical tension in mentorship involves supporting students as they navigate educational systems that may not reflect their lived experiences while empowering them to resist and transform those systems. Yosso's (2005) concept of navigational capital exemplifies how students leverage their skills and networks to move through institutions that were not designed with them in mind. For instance, a student from a low-income background may have developed strong problem-solving skills to overcome financial and academic hurdles; a mentor can acknowledge and build on these skills while helping the student strategize ways to challenge unfair policies or practices they may encounter. Mentors should guide students in recognizing that resilience is not merely about enduring but about actively resisting inequities and leveraging their experiences to drive change. This approach helps shift mentorship from simply helping students adapt to an environment to empowering them to critique and reshape it. By fostering this mindset, mentors contribute to a student's sense of agency, positioning them as proactive changemakers who can advocate for inclusivity and justice within higher education and their broader communities.

Calling Out Deficit Perspectives: Imposter Syndrome and Racelighting

Navigating academic spaces can involve grappling with a phenomenon referred to as "imposter syndrome," especially for students of color. **Imposter syndrome** is characterized by persistent self-doubt and fear of being exposed as a "fraud," even despite evident accomplishments. For students of color, these feelings are often exacerbated by systemic racism and a lack of positive representation within educational institutions, which have delivered racialized messages that make people of color second guess their experiences, abilities, and who they can trust. Research indicates that imposter syndrome is linked to various mental health challenges, including anxiety, depression, and stress (Cokley et al., 2013; Parkman, 2016).

First-generation students of color, in particular, may struggle with imposter syndrome due to the dual pressures of navigating college as pioneers within their families and contending with racialized stereotypes that question their academic legitimacy (Le, 2019). This phenomenon is compounded by institutional narratives that fail to recognize the systemic barriers contributing to these feelings. Recognizing and addressing imposter syndrome in educational programs can help mitigate its negative impacts and support students in developing a sense of belonging and academic confidence (Luedke, 2017).

To resist deficit-based perspectives, it is essential for educators and institutions to honestly acknowledge the structural origins of imposter syndrome to counter racelighting (Wood & Harris, 2024). Reframing and interrogating narratives to highlight the inherent strengths of students, rather than viewing them as needing to "overcome" internalized deficiencies, *shifts the focus from individual shortcomings to institutional responsibilities.*

Critical Issues and Considerations

As the landscape of higher education continues to evolve, certain issues seem to remain persistently relevant and demand ongoing attention. Consider how developmental and antiracist frameworks can support your understanding of these concerns.

Navigating Institutional Challenges

The effects of the COVID-19 pandemic shed light on and exacerbated existing structural inequities faced by racially and ethnically marginalized communities in higher education. Iruka et al. (2022) identify COVID-19 as a **"racial macro stressor"** that intensified pre-existing disparities, such as economic precarity, limited access to technology, and disruptions in educational continuity. During the pandemic, students from Black, Latine, and Native American backgrounds disproportionately faced campus closures and had fewer resources for online learning compared to their White counterparts. This digital divide, marked by unreliable internet access and inadequate technology, further hindered academic progress and widened achievement gaps, reinforcing systemic inequities.

Furthermore, REM (Racially and Ethnically Marginalized) college students encountered compounded challenges related to employment instability, housing insecurity, and increased exposure to race-related trauma during the pandemic. These stressors not only affected academic outcomes but also impacted mental health and overall well-being. The dual crises of structural racism and COVID-19 underscore the necessity for antiracist policies that address both immediate and deep-rooted inequities. Institutions must continue to prioritize strategies that bolster student support systems, ensuring resilience is not just expected of individuals but built into the structural fabric of higher education.

Bias and Its Impact on Development

Bias within educational environments, whether overt or subtle, significantly impacts student development and academic performance. **Microaggressions**, as highlighted in recent research by Ogunyemi et al. (2020), are one such manifestation of bias that students may encounter. These brief, often unintentional discriminatory comments or actions convey negative or prejudiced attitudes toward marginalized groups and accumulate over time to create a hostile educational climate.

Developmental psychology illustrates that chronic exposure to microaggressions can erode a student's sense of safety and belonging, which are essential for fostering cognitive and emotional growth. Prolonged experiences of bias can lead to heightened stress responses, adversely affecting students' focus, motivation, and overall mental health. This ongoing psychological toll can result in diminished academic engagement and hindered personal development.

For child and adolescent development professionals in higher education, it is essential to recognize how these dynamics play out within institutional contexts. Addressing bias involves identifying and acknowledging its varied manifestations, assessing its effects on student well-being, and developing targeted strategies to counteract these impacts. This work extends beyond reinforcing student resilience to actively challenging and changing the systemic structures that maintain and reproduce such inequities (Ogunyemi et al., 2020).

Campus Climate Assessments

Campus climate assessments are essential tools for identifying areas of growth and equity needs within higher education institutions. These assessments should employ both qualitative and quantitative methods to capture the comprehensive lived experiences of students. By framing these assessments through a developmental and antiracist lens, professionals can better understand how systemic structures impact student development and make informed recommendations for change (Contreras & Contreras, 2015).

One critical quantitative metric in these assessments is the **DFW rate** – the percentage of students who receive a grade of D or F or withdraw from a course. High DFW rates indicate courses where students could face challenges with the course itself. Research has shown that large gateway courses often have higher DFW rates compared to smaller classes (Roberts et al., 2018). These findings suggest that course structure and support mechanisms play essential roles in student success.

By integrating DFW rate analysis with **qualitative data** such as *student testimonials and focus group insights*, institutions can gain a comprehensive understanding of where targeted interventions are needed. *Qualitative data collection plays a crucial role in uncovering the nuanced challenges that students face*, which may not be reflected in quantitative measures alone. For example, focus group discussions can reveal specific barriers to success in foundational courses, such as teaching methods, policy, or course content that may not align with students' learning needs or cultural backgrounds. When paired with DFW analysis, these insights enable institutions to implement tailored strategies, such as supplemental instruction, increased academic advising, or pedagogical adjustments, to create more inclusive learning environments.

Note that some so-called "traditional" metrics are increasingly seen as inadequate for assessing the complete picture of the experience of today's students, particularly marginalized populations. While these measures may point to persistence, they do not necessarily indicate college completion. Students may, for instance, be more likely to attend part-time, work over 20 hours per week, and/or experience longer time-to-degree averages (Contreras & Contreras, 2015).

These realities challenge the utility of conventional metrics and highlight the importance of developing more comprehensive measures that reflect the diverse experiences of today's college students. Scholars advocate for tracking additional data points to provide a clearer, more nuanced picture of student success. This expanded approach not only captures persistence but also reflects the structural challenges students face (Contreras & Contreras, 2015).

Incorporating *multiple measures into a broad campus climate assessment* ensures that data-driven, equitable strategies can be developed to support students effectively. A more holistic approach helps build academic environments where students of all backgrounds have equitable opportunities to succeed, aligning with the antiracist and developmental principles foundational to the Antiracist Praxis Model outlined in Chapter 1.

These concepts of affirming and sustaining student identity, aligning professional practices with antiracist principles, and addressing critical issues and considerations reflect many elements of the MMDLE. They can be approached in an organized way using the Antiracist Praxis Model. To illustrate these ideas, we will guide you through an analysis based on a real-life university setting. Please follow along, and at the end of the chapter, you will have the chance to apply the model yourself with reflect and practice activities.

Practical Example: California's First Black-Serving Institution (BSI)

In June 2024, Sacramento State became California's first BSI, a significant milestone for the university, which, at the time of this writing, enrolls the largest number of Black students within the California State University (CSU) system. This example explores the university's journey toward this designation, focusing on initiatives led by President Dr. Luke Wood, who championed programs such as the Black Honors College (BHC) from the outset of his tenure with the goal of creating an inclusive, supportive educational environment (Hubert, 2024).

Background and Context

Sacramento State's designation as a BSI was formalized through a resolution by the California State Assembly, recognizing the university's efforts to increase enrollment and improve outcomes for Black students, who comprise approximately 6% of the student body (Hubert, 2024). Dr. Wood, an equity-focused leader and Sacramento State alumnus, spearheaded foundational initiatives such as the BHC to enhance academic and personal development opportunities for Black students and foster an inclusive campus climate (Hubert, 2024).

Institutional Policies, Campus Climate, and Student Voice

Analyzing Sacramento State's policies through the MMDLE reveals the interactions of institutional context with student experiences. The creation of the BHC exemplifies proactive measures that can be viewed with the MMDLE's emphasis on inclusive practices. However, to consider the many perspectives within the MMDLE, it is essential to consider student voice. Regularly incorporating feedback from students allows institutions to adapt policies and practices to their evolving needs. Professionals can regularly reflect on questions such as: How are student perspectives gathered and integrated into policy-making? Are there systems in place to ensure feedback leads to meaningful change?

Students have reported mixed experiences; while many appreciate the new programs, challenges such as microaggressions and slower responses to incidents of bias persist. This underscores the need for institutions to build robust, transparent, and efficient bias response systems that are regularly assessed. For ongoing reflection, professionals can find ways to ask: Are current measures effectively addressing students' reported concerns? Are students part of the dialogue in shaping these protocols?

Mentorship, Intersectionality, and Support Structures

Before his arrival, Black students at Sacramento State faced limited mentorship tailored to their specific needs (Hubert, 2024). Recognizing this, Dr. Wood's administration developed programs like the Black Success Initiative, which provides mentorship and support that consider the intersectional identities of students. Intersectionality, the interconnected nature of race, gender, socioeconomic status, and other identity markers, plays a critical role in shaping individual experiences. To create effective mentorship, professionals should reflect: Are mentoring programs acknowledging and addressing the intersectional challenges students face? Are mentors equipped with the skills to support students' multifaceted identities?

The goal of the Black Success Initiative and mentorship programs is for students gain targeted academic and emotional support. To sustain this, institutions should periodically evaluate these programs for effectiveness. Mentors should receive continuous training that integrates culturally responsive approaches to the systemic barriers impacting students' development.

Developmental Theory and Holistic Support

From a developmental perspective, Sacramento State's approach under Dr. Wood's leadership highlights the importance of creating interactive support structures that nurture resilience and academic growth. This reflects placing value on the bioecological model's focus on context and process. To apply this insight, educators and administrators can ask: Are support systems providing consistent, long-term benefits? Are they responsive to feedback from the student body?

Reflective practice includes examining whether students feel genuinely represented and supported, which requires continuous dialogue between students, mentors, and university staff. Professionals can regularly consider: How do mentorship programs and policies impact students' developmental outcomes? What adjustments can be made to better support holistic development?

Analysis: Applying Antiracist Frameworks

The MMDLE, Antiracist Praxis Model, and other frameworks in this book can be used to consider and discuss Sacramento State's journey towards the creation (and now maintenance of) a Black-Serving Institution. The BHC and mentorship programs could be used to consider significance of embedding antiracist strategies within institutional structures. As all of these efforts likely remain dynamic and responsive, they give us opportunities to reflect. Reflective questions include: Are these programs integrated throughout the university, or do they operate in isolation? Are faculty and staff engaged in ongoing training to support antiracist work?

For professionals using the Antiracist Praxis Model, regular reflection, and adaptation is an integral part of that process. Consider whether there are avenues for student advocacy and leadership within these initiatives. Institutions should ultimately create spaces where students can contribute to the development and evaluation of programs, reinforcing their voices as agents of change.

Cautions and Continuous Improvement

While Sacramento State's initiatives mark substantial progress, potential pitfalls include the risk of relying too heavily on select programs or individuals. Institutions should reflect: Are these efforts sustainable and supported by the broader university infrastructure? That is, move your gaze to the systems-level of racism. What is happening there? Regular assessments, transparent communication, and an inclusive feedback loop involving students and faculty are essential for maintaining and scaling successful initiatives.

Finally, mentorship can be monitored to ensure it remains effective and inclusive. Professionals can ask: Are mentors and students participating in ongoing discussions about intersectionality and systemic issues? Are there mechanisms to adapt mentorship approaches based on evolving needs?

Conclusion

Sacramento State's journey to becoming a Black-Serving Institution highlights the interplay of student voice, institutional policies, mentorship, and intersectional understanding in fostering an inclusive environment. This example demonstrates the helpfulness of developmental frameworks like the MMDLE and the Antiracist Praxis Model, illustrating the importance of ongoing reflection, student engagement, and continuous improvement. By applying these principles, future professionals can contribute to creating equitable, transformative educational spaces that respond to the complex realities of student experiences.

Antiracist Professional Identity Development

Developing an antiracist professional identity requires more than theoretical understanding; it calls for active reflection, structured practice, and continuous learning. **Using the lens of the MMDLE and the Antiracist Praxis Model** can help professionals examine how various factors – such as institutional context and campus climate – shape their work, highlighting both strengths and areas for growth. Engaging in mentorship, feedback, and professional development builds the "muscle memory" necessary for effective, real-world application. Incorporating feedback from peers and institutional assessments supports ongoing reflection, ensuring practices remain inclusive, adaptable, and responsive. Sustaining this commitment by revisiting goals and refining strategies fosters personal growth and meaningful, systemic change.

Structured practice, such as working through case studies, critical questions, and guided activities, offers a controlled space for professionals to apply these antiracist frameworks. This approach enables individuals to test strategies, reflect on outcomes, and gain valuable insights without the pressures of real-time decision-making. Engaging in these exercises sharpens the ability to recognize biases, translate theory into practice, and implement antiracist principles effectively. As readers move into the Reflect and Practice Activities section, they are encouraged to fully engage in these activities to deepen their understanding, build confidence, and prepare to seamlessly integrate these concepts into their professional work.

Reflect and Practice Activities

The following section contains activities that can be completed independently or with others, including a case study, critical questions, campus climate equity audit, an interview, and asset mapping activities.

Case Study Analysis: Grading Policies

Read the fictional case study below about how a university department is grappling with inclusive grading policies to support a diverse, "post-traditional" student body. While the department and individuals in the story are fictional, the scenario reflects real challenges faced in higher education settings. As you read, consider the complexities of balancing equity, academic rigor, and systemic change. After reading, you will use the Antiracist Praxis Model to analyze the department's approach and develop strategies for addressing the identified inequities.

Background

At Metro State University, a (fictional) public institution known for its diverse and "post-traditional" student population, many students are from racially minoritized backgrounds and are first-generation college attendees, who juggle other significant commitments alongside their studies. However, the social sciences department still operates under participation and grading policies in their fieldwork classes that assume students have ample time to focus exclusively on their academic work. This disconnect has led to growing concerns among students, especially working parents, who report feeling unsupported and unfairly evaluated by rigid practices.

The student organization, Advocates for Equity in Education (AEE), recently conducted a survey that highlighted these issues. The findings showed that students with caregiving responsibilities, working students, and those from underrepresented backgrounds faced higher levels of stress and lower academic performance due to grading policies that did not take their circumstances into account. The AEE presented these findings at a student-faculty forum, advocating for more inclusive grading practices, such as flexible deadlines and multiple formats for participation in fieldwork classes.

Dr. Patel, an early-career faculty member who attended the forum, was moved by the stories shared by her students. She realized that, despite her best efforts to create a supportive classroom, the department's fieldwork course policies limited her ability to accommodate the needs of her students effectively. While some faculty members expressed interest in revisiting these policies, others raised concerns about maintaining academic standards and fairness.

The department chair, Dr. Simmons, stated that any major policy changes would need to be carefully considered before being adopted more widely. However, Dr. Patel is eager to start making small changes in her own classes and to support students in their push for a more flexible fieldwork course and grading policies that reflects the realities of their post-traditional student body.

Analyze

To analyze the case study, use both your understanding of the **Multicontextual Model for Diverse Learning Environments** and the **Antiracist Praxis Model** to guide your approach. These models provide structured ways to identify, understand, and develop solutions for inequities in educational settings. You can use the instructions below individually or to guide a small group discussion.

- **Step 1: Identify Inequities**
  Begin by reading the case study thoroughly. Identify the specific inequities present in the situation and discuss their impacts. Consider background information that is important for understanding the context, such as who is affected by these inequities and the key figures involved. Make note of the root causes and contributing factors.
- **Step 2: Perspective Exploration**
  Examine the different perspectives of those involved in the case. Reflect on the experiences and motivations of various stakeholders, including students, faculty members, and administrators. Consider how each group's background and experiences influence their view of the situation. Discuss how these perspectives contribute to or challenge the existing inequities.
- **Step 3: Ecological Analysis**
  Analyze the processes and broader contexts that affect the situation. Think about how different layers of influence – such as institutional policies,

departmental norms, and cultural expectations – interact to reinforce or challenge the inequities. Discuss how these layers align with the ecological systems model, focusing on the interconnected nature of these influences.
- **Step 4: Identify Community Readiness**
Research or discuss how similar challenges have been approached at other institutions. Reflect on what has been tried before and the outcomes. Use this information to assess the readiness of the current community for change. Consider the reactions and responses that previous efforts have generated to better understand what is feasible in this context.
- **Step 5: Brainstorm Potential Actions**
Generate ideas for potential actions that could address the identified inequities. Start with short-term, actionable steps that could be implemented relatively quickly. Then, brainstorm longer-term strategies that might require more time or resources but could lead to sustainable change. Aim to identify solutions that promote equity and antiracism.
- **Step 6: Identify Supportive Resources**
Think about what resources could support the implementation of the actions you've brainstormed. Identify both knowledge-based resources, such as mentors, professional organizations, and educational materials, as well as material resources, like funding, technology, or collaborative tools. Discuss how these resources could be leveraged effectively.
- **Step 7: Reflect on Potential Barriers**
Consider potential barriers to implementing the actions you have identified. Analyze how factors such as resistance from stakeholders, logistical challenges, or resource limitations might impact the feasibility of each proposed action. Discuss strategies for overcoming these barriers and how they might shape your approach.
- **Step 8: Develop Immediate and Long-Term Personal Action Steps**
Based on your analysis, outline a plan of action that includes both immediate and long-term steps. Identify specific actions that can be taken right away and those that require more time to implement. Ensure that your plan is realistic and considers the resources and barriers you previously identified.
- **Step 9: Reflect and Adapt**
Reflection is a crucial part of this process. Think about how the actions taken might impact the broader system and what adjustments may be necessary as the situation evolves. Analyze your observations, responses, and outcomes to refine your understanding and strategies. Incorporate continuous feedback to adapt and improve your approach over time.

Critical Questions

The reflection questions below encourage your critical thinking and engagement with the chapter's content. In response to the prompts below, you can free-write rapid reactions, write longer papers supported by related literature, and/or formulate strategies through small group discussion in class.

1. How can understanding the **Multicontextual Model for Diverse Learning Environments** shape your approach to how you view your work in your professional setting?
2. Reflect on how *racelighting* may manifest in higher education and its potential effects on racially minoritized students. What strategies can mentors use to disrupt these subtle forms of racialized gaslighting and foster an environment that affirms students' identities and accomplishments?
3. Pick an *antiracist strategy* you would like to implement. What systemic, institutional, and interpersonal challenges might arise when implementing this strategy in higher education, and how can you prepare to simultaneously navigate these challenges while maintaining a commitment to equity?
4. Reflect on your *personal biases and positionality*. How do these aspects influence your interactions and decisions in your work, and what practical, actionable steps will you take to align your actions with antiracist principles?

Other Activity Ideas

Campus Climate Equity Audit

Engage in a campus or workplace climate equity audit to apply antiracist developmental principles in a practical context. Begin by gathering qualitative data through focus groups and interviews with peers, colleagues, faculty, or staff to gain insights into their experiences with diversity, equity, and inclusion. Develop and distribute surveys to assess the broader perceptions of the climate in your environment, focusing on areas such as inclusivity, support, and systemic equity. Once data is collected, analyze it to identify trends, strengths, and areas needing improvement. Use this analysis to create targeted recommendations that address these areas, aligning them with the developmental needs and experiences of racially and culturally diverse individuals. This activity will help you understand how institutional culture impacts development and equity, setting a foundation for meaningful change.

Antiracist Praxis Interview

Interview a mentor, supervisor, or experienced colleague to explore their personal experiences in supporting development and promoting antiracism. Focus on understanding how they navigate challenges, advocate for antiracist practices, and integrate developmental theories into their work. Take note of strategies they employ and their reflections on lessons learned over time. After conducting the interview, take time to reflect on how their insights can inform your own professional approach. Consider what practices resonate with your values and how you might adapt their strategies in your work. This activity emphasizes personal connection and reflection, fostering a deeper understanding of how antiracist principles can be embodied in real-world professional practice.

Mapping Systems and Identifying Assets

Participate in a mapping exercise to explore the different systems that impact development and equity in your specific professional or academic context. Identify key elements such as institutional policies, local community resources, support programs, and networks. Map out how these components interact and influence development, identifying assets within these systems that can be leveraged to support antiracist and developmental goals. This exercise will deepen your understanding of how systemic interactions shape opportunities and outcomes, guiding you to craft strategies that align with both developmental and antiracist practices.

Chapter Summary

- Shift to antiracist frameworks like MMDLE to support racially diverse populations.
- Recognize and address intersecting identities and systemic power structures.
- Cultivate critical consciousness to challenge and disrupt inequitable practices.
- Build social justice resilience and promote empathy and problem-solving.
- Implement identity-responsive mentorship to reduce the "diversity tax" on faculty and staff of color.
- Reframe imposter syndrome as a structural issue to support student confidence and belonging.
- Foster inclusive campus climates through intentional policies and regular assessments.
- Engage in reflective practice and seek feedback to ensure adaptable, effective strategies.
- Participate in structured practice activities (case studies, mapping, reflection) to apply antiracist frameworks effectively.

Recommended Resources

The following books, articles, and other resources may help you deepen your understanding of antiracism in higher education professional contexts.

- The MMDLE model can be found in: Hurtado, S., Alvarez, C. L., Guillermo-Wann, C., Cuellar, M., & Arellano, L. (2012). A model for diverse learning

environments. In J. C. Smart & M. B. Paulsen (Eds.), *Higher education: Handbook of theory and research* (Vol. 27, pp. 41–122). Springer. https://doi.org/10.1007/978-94-007-2950-6_2
- Solórzano, D. G., & Huber, L. P. (2020). *Racial microaggressions: Using critical race theory to respond to everyday racism.* Teachers College Press.
- Race Forward and Facing Race: A National Conference. https://facingrace.raceforward.org/
- National Association of Diversity Officers in Higher Education (NADOHE). https://www.nadohe.org/
- Cabrera, N. L. (2024). *Whiteness in the ivory tower: Why don't we notice the white students sitting together in the quad?* Teachers College Press.

References

Bronfenbrenner, U., & Morris, P. (2006). The bioecological model of human development. In R. M. Lerner & W. Damon (Eds.), *Handbook of child psychology: Vol. 1. Theoretical models of human development* (6th ed., pp. 793–828). Wiley.

Cokley, K., McClain, S., Enciso, A., & Martinez, M. (2013). An examination of the impact of minority status stress and impostor feelings on the mental health of diverse ethnic minority college students. *Journal of Multicultural Counseling and Development, 41*(2), 82–95.

Contreras, F., & Contreras, G. J. (2015). Raising the bar for Hispanic serving institutions: An analysis of college completion and success rates. *Journal of Hispanic Higher Education, 14*(2), 151–170.

Crenshaw, K. (1991). Mapping the margins: Intersectionality, identity politics, and violence against women of color. *Stanford Law Review, 43*(6), 1241–1299. https://doi.org/10.2307/1229039

Ferreira van Leer, K., Gonzalez, A., Razo Soto, M., Songs of the Hummingbird, & Mariposas con Voces. (2024). *Latine undergraduate students indicate need for greater Latine cultural representation within HSIs* (Research Brief No. 2024-01). Using Our Voices to Transform HSIs Collaborative.

Freire, P. (1970). *Pedagogy of the oppressed.* Herder and Herder.

Garcia, G. A., Núñez, A. M., & Sansone, V. A. (2019). Toward a multidimensional conceptual framework for understanding "servingness" in Hispanic-serving institutions: A synthesis of the research. *Review of Educational Research, 89*(5), 745–784.

Glowacki-Dudka, M. (2019). How to engage nontraditional adult learners through popular education in higher education. *Adult Learning, 30*(2), 84–86.

Gonzalez, M., Kokozos, M., Byrd, C. M., & McKee, K. E. (2020). Critical positive youth development: A framework for centering critical consciousness. *Journal of Youth Development, 15*(6), 24–43.

Gulley, N. Y. (2021). Challenging assumptions: 'Contemporary students,' 'nontraditional students,' 'adult learners,' 'post-traditional,' 'new traditional'. *SCHOLE: A Journal of Leisure Studies and Recreation Education, 36*(1–2), 4–10.

Gurin, P., Dey, E. L., Hurtado, S., & Gurin, G. (2002). Diversity and higher education: Theory and impact on educational outcomes. *Harvard Educational Review, 72*(3), 330–366. https://doi.org/10.17763/haer.72.3.01151786u134n051

Hubert, C. (June 6, 2024). Sacramento State designated as Black-Serving Institution. *California State University, Sacramento Newsroom.* https://www.csus.edu/news/newsroom/stories/2024/6/black-serving-institution.html

Hurtado, S., Alvarez, C. L., Guillermo-Wann, C., Cuellar, M., & Arellano, L. (2012). A model for diverse learning environments. In J. C. Smart & M. B. Paulsen (Eds.), *Higher education: Handbook of theory and research* (Vol. 27, pp. 41–122). Springer. https://doi.org/10.1007/978-94-007-2950-6_2

Iloh, C. (2018). Toward a new model of college "choice" for a twenty-first-century context. *Harvard Educational Review, 88*(2), 227–244.

Iruka, I. U., Gardner-Neblett, N., Telfer, N. A., Ibekwe-Okafor, N., Curenton, S. M., Sims, J., ... & Neblett, E. W. (2022). Effects of racism on child development: Advancing antiracist developmental science. *Annual Review of Developmental Psychology, 4*(1), 109–132.

Kuh, G. D. (2008). Excerpt from high-impact educational practices: What they are, who has access to them, and why they matter. *Association of American Colleges and Universities, 14*(3), 28–29.

Le, L. (2019). Unpacking the imposter syndrome and mental health as a person of color first generation college student within institutions of higher education. *McNair Research Journal SJSU, 15*(1), 5.

Luedke, C. L. (2017). Person first, student second: Staff and administrators of color supporting students of color authentically in higher education. *Journal of College Student Development, 58*(1), 37–52.

Navarette, L. (2021). *The overlooked working majority: Supporting working adult learners at California community colleges with intentionality* (Doctoral dissertation). University of California, Davis. ProQuest ID: Navarette_ucdavis_0029D_20634. Merritt ID: ark:/13030/m5sj8bnq. https://escholarship.org/uc/item/740055qn

Ogunyemi, D., Clare, C., Astudillo, Y. M., Marseille, M., Manu, E., & Kim, S. (2020). Microaggressions in the learning environment: A systematic review. *Journal of Diversity in Higher Education, 13*(2), 97–119. https://doi.org/10.1037/dhe0000107

Parkman, A. (2016). The imposter phenomenon in higher education: Incidence and impact. *Journal of Higher Education Theory and Practice, 16*(1), 51–57.

Rendón, L. I. (2006). Reconceptualizing success for underserved students in higher education. *NACADA Journal, 26*(1), 12–24.

Rendón, L. I., & Cantú, N. (2009). *Sentipensante (sensing/thinking) pedagogy: Educating for wholeness, social justice, and liberation.* Routledge.

Roberts, J. A., Olcott, A. N., McLean, N. M., Baker, G. S., & Möller, A. (2018). Demonstrating the impact of classroom transformation on the inequality in DFW rates ("D" or "F" grade or withdraw) for first-time freshmen, females, and underrepresented minorities through a decadal study of introductory geology courses. *Journal of Geoscience Education, 66*(4), 304–318.

Shumaker, R., & Wood, J. L. (2016). Understanding First-generation community college students: An analysis of covariance examining use of, access to, and efficacy regarding institutionally offered services. *Community College Enterprise, 22*(2), 9–16.

Suzuki, S., Johnson, S. K., & Ferreira van Leer, K. (2023). Situating critical consciousness within the developmental system: Insights from the phenomenological variant of ecological systems theory. In L. Rapa & E. Godfrey (Eds.), *Critical consciousness: Expanding theory and measurement* (pp. 41–62). Cambridge University Press.

Wood, J. L., & Frank Harris III. (2024). Racelighting Black, indigenous and people of color in education: A conceptual framework. *Equality, Diversity and Inclusion: An International Journal, 43*(3), 400–409.

Yosso, T. J. (2005). Whose culture has capital? A critical race theory discussion of community cultural wealth. *Race Ethnicity and Education, 8*(1), 69–91.

Chapter 5

Antiracist Approaches for Allied Health Professionals

Introduction

Similar to teachers and social workers, many allied health professionals feel a calling to care for others. Also like teachers, many health professionals are focused on supporting individuals, though in this case the goal is promoting health and well-being. Providing individual health care can be hugely rewarding and meaningful for both the professional and the client. Many movies and television shows present glorified images of how health professionals, particularly doctors and nurses, engage in individual, heroic acts of healing in acute care settings such as hospitals. While these representations can be inspirational, they do not tell the whole story. Unfortunately, some patient care interactions in health settings are fraught with implicit bias, stereotyping, and discrimination. Due to racial discrimination, individuals from minoritized racial groups often receive lower quality healthcare and differential treatment compared to their White peers with similar access to health care (Smedley et al., 2003). Thus, allied health professionals must engage in ongoing self-reflection and take actions to combat racism at the interpersonal level.

Despite the individual narratives common in media, health professionals always operate as part of interdependent teams within larger institutions. Similar to tackling misconceptions about individualistic efforts in the teaching profession we explored in Chapter 3, health professionals must analyze how health care systems have codified racist, sexist, classist, and other discriminatory practices. For example, consider how the quality and quantity of health care an individual receives is determined by whether they have health insurance and what tests or treatments the provider can get reimbursed by a specific insurance plan. Even uninsured and underinsured adolescents ages 13–17 have worse self-reported health and decreased preventive care utilization, with poor health status persisting long term, than those who are wealthier with excellent health insurance (Horne et al., 2022). Our health insurance system in the United States is just one way classist policies contribute to health inequities.

DOI: 10.4324/9781003374176-6

In particular, racism and racist policies are increasingly recognized by researchers as key drivers of poor health outcomes in the United States (Jones, 2000). Racism directly and indirectly contributes to **health disparities**, which are preventable differences in health outcomes that affect socially disadvantaged or marginalized populations. It is important to note that racial health disparities are not due to racial differences, since race is a social construct, not a biological one. So then, how does systemic racism cause differences in individual and community health outcomes? And, why are the effects of racism so prevalent in a system staffed by professionals dedicated to healing and caring?

While allied health professionals represent a wide variety of roles in health service delivery, they share a commitment to improving the health of others. Our health care system today is complex, and requires the support of a multitude of professionals who have important roles in promoting the health of individuals, communities, and our nation. While some roles, such as nurses, have been around for hundreds of years, others, like community health workers or health promoters, are relatively new and evolving. Regardless of their specific role, health professionals must collectively adopt a variety of strategies to combat racism and the effects of racism on health.

As a result of increasing data on racial health disparities, the health professions are starting to embrace new, ecologically-based theoretical frameworks, such as the **social determinants of health (SDOH)**. The SDOH are nonmedical factors that can influence health outcomes (Centers for Disease Control and Prevention [CDC], 2024) and prompt us to consider the health influences of where and how we are born, live, study, work, play, and age. Racial disparities in health outcomes reveal how racist policies and the environments created by these policies deprive specific groups and communities of health-protective resources and opportunities in various life contexts.

This paradigm shift in understanding the socio-environmental contributors to health outcomes is still in process, as some health professionals still attribute poor health solely to individual behaviors, or "unhealthy lifestyles." While behaviors, like smoking or eating a high-sugar diet certainly contribute to developing cardiovascular disease or diabetes, behaviors alone do not account for disparities in health outcomes. Health researchers and providers are starting to explore how stressors such as racism and other forms of discrimination negatively impact internal biological processes. Stress can lead to physiological **weathering**, also known as increased **allostatic load** (McEwen & Stellar, 1993), which can contribute to poor physical and mental health outcomes. We will explore these processes and how health professionals can try to counteract them, in the section on critical issues and actions.

In this chapter, we will guide you in analyzing the myriad ways racism affects health and in learning antiracist strategies that allied health professionals can employ in a variety of health care settings. Antiracist strategies include reflecting on explicit and implicit biases, adopting **cultural humility**, **disrupting**

microaggressions, using developmental approaches to **cultivating protective factors** in children, adolescents, and families, and **building power** within communities to cultivate community belonging and "agency" for collective advocacy toward improved conditions.

This chapter's key features include:

- Health Disparities
- Applying the Bioecological Model to the Social Determinants of Health
- Physiological Effects of Racism
- Implicit Bias and Microaggressions in Healthcare
- Strategies for Addressing Racism
- Developing an Antiracist Health Professional Identity
- Reflect and Practice Activities
- Recommended Resources

Applying Key Concepts and Theoretical Frameworks to Health

Health Disparities

Health disparities can result from a variety of factors in addition to racism, including other forms of discrimination, poverty, environmental threats, inadequate access to care, individual and behavioral factors, and educational inequities. The COVID-19 pandemic offers one example of racial health disparities. Data showed that Black, Latine, American Indian or Alaska Native, and Native Hawaiian or other Pacific Islander people experienced higher rates of COVID-19 cases and death compared to White people (Hill & Artiga, 2022). These disparities in illness (morbidity) and death (mortality) rates illustrate how structural inequities in health and health care quality, along with social and economic factors, placed people of color at higher risk. There were multiple factors driving this disparity, such as people of color being more likely to experience higher exposure in many "essential worker" roles, living in multi-generational, shared housing where they could not isolate from others, and being uninsured or underinsured so they could not access quality health care (Duong et al., 2023).

Social Determinants of Health

The SDOH represent the conditions in the environments in which we are born, live, work, play, worship, as well as age (CDC, 2024). The five domains of the SDOH are (1) healthcare access and quality, (2) education access and quality, (3) social and community context, (4) economic stability, and (5) neighborhood and built environment. Racism and related SDOH affect life expectancy. In one study, African Americans' life expectancy averaged 75.7 years, while the highest – for Asian/Pacific Islanders – was 12 years higher, at 87.7 years (Singh et al., 2017). In addition, Black infants have 2.3 higher mortality than White infants (Singh et al., 2017). Researchers and health advocates have presented data suggesting that where you live – specifically your zip code – is predictive of your life expectancy (Robert Wood Johnson Foundation, 2001–2024). This is a result of government-imposed policies that established residential racial segregation starting in the 1930s, including racial zoning (called "redlining") where people of color, and in particular Black and Latine communities, were forced to live in designated areas which were severely under-resourced, could not secure home loans, and were excluded from homeownership in White suburbs (Rothstein, 2017).

Due to the pervasive effects of structural and institutional racism, health outcomes are worse for people who grew up or live in previously redlined neighborhoods. This includes increased rates of chronic conditions, injury, infectious disease, and childhood lead poisoning, and worse mental health, maternal and infant health, and general health outcomes (Swope et al., 2022). In addition, children who grow up in previously redlined neighborhoods experience significantly lower levels of educational attainment, higher poverty, and reduced income as adults (Aaronson et al., 2023), which can contribute to reduced access to health care. In an era marked by the effects of climate change, it is important to note that people living in previously redlined areas are more likely to experience flood risk and extreme heat (Conzelmann et al., 2022) and heat-related illness (Swope et al., 2022) compared to those living in wealthier, more tree-lined neighborhoods. In essence, racist policies have created social and environmental contexts that contribute to poor health outcomes as much, if not more than individual behaviors. Now, we will explore how the **bioecological model** (Bronfenbrenner & Morris, 2006) informs analysis of SDOH.

The Social Determinants of Health and Bioecological Model

In Chapter 1, we learned how the bioecological model facilitates our understanding of the processes between an individual and their context, emphasizing interactions between the person and their environment that become increasingly complex over time. Applying the bioecological model to health helps us critically analyze health influences within a socio-cultural and antiracist context. A person's health status is influenced by a variety of factors, including genetic predispositions or risks, health behaviors (like smoking), and SDOH. Within each SDOH domain, we can find conditions that can be supportive to individual and community health, or can contribute to worse health outcomes. We will explore each domain of the SDOH as they relate to Bronfenbrenner's bioecological model.

In the **Microsystem** – daily interactions in the immediate environment, such as your family, friends, school, and neighborhood – the SDOH domains of education access and quality, social and community context, and neighborhood and built environment come into play. Children and adolescents may enjoy a secure home, school, and neighborhood environment where they feel safe, have parks to play in, and are positively encouraged by teachers – all of which can contribute to good health outcomes. Conversely, children and youth of color may experience stressful discrimination at school that leads them to dropping out, substandard living conditions that increase their risk of health conditions like asthma, and a lack of access to fresh fruits and vegetables or safe places to play, which may contribute to obesity.

In the **Mesosystem**, which connects the various parts of your microsystem, all the SDOH domains can intersect. For example, consider how families' economic stability can affect children's housing quality, neighborhood context, and experience at school. If parents are financially secure, their children are more likely to attend a school with better resources, have access to healthier foods, parks, and athletic facilities. Likewise, parents will have better health insurance and more time to take their children to preventive healthcare visits. However, if parents are struggling financially, their children are more likely to experience a more stressful and under-resourced neighborhood, educational, and healthcare environment.

The **Exosystem** involves the broader social systems that you might not interact with directly but still impact your life, such as parents' workplaces, community services, and local government policies. These social systems can cut across the different SDOH domains, especially the social and community context and economic stability. For instance, if parents have a work environment protected by a policy requiring paid sick leave, they are more likely to take their child to preventive or acute care health appointments, positively affecting children's health status. If the school district or county has policies or funds for comprehensive school health programs, children are more likely to receive supportive health care from a licensed school nurse or social worker during the school day. However, if parents are working multiple, stressful part-time jobs without any employment benefits or protections, they may not have the time or energy to navigate community services or the healthcare system. Children and adolescents may not get preventive health care, such as sports physicals, vaccines, eye glasses, or dental care, which can negatively affect their health outcomes, level of educational attainment, and recreational or employment opportunities.

The **Macrosystem** encompasses the larger societal influences that shape your environment, such as cultural values, economic conditions, and political systems. For example, culturally "normalized" values of racism and xenophobia after the "9/11" World Trade Center bombing may have influenced the SDOH of social and community context and economic stability for some Muslim community members. This, in turn, impacts other SDOH such as education and housing. In this example, children of Muslim immigrants who struggle to find secure employment and housing may be more likely to live in substandard housing, attend under-resourced schools, and receive inadequate health care. The racism and anti-Islamic attitudes that the whole family may experience could contribute to high levels of stress, with resulting anxiety, depression, and/or physical symptoms. Conversely, when political, organizational, and social systems enact a social contract supportive of children and families through programs such as guaranteed income or universal health care, families' economic stability, educational quality, and healthcare access may improve. In this way, society's codified systems can contribute to improved health status and health outcomes.

Multiple SDOH can also be influenced in the **Chronosystem**, which considers how life transitions and socio-historical events affect your health and development. Major events like moving to a new neighborhood or school, or significant societal changes such as the COVID-19 pandemic can all play a role in shaping children's and adolescents' health over time. For example, due to some politicians erroneously blaming China and Asian people in general for the COVID-19 pandemic, many Asian Americans experienced racism during this worldwide socio-historical event (Ruiz et al., 2023). As a result of significantly elevated racial discrimination during the COVID-19 pandemic, one study found that 40% of Asian Americans reported an increase in anxiety, depressive symptoms, and sleep difficulties, all of which can contribute to worse physical and mental health outcomes (Lee & Waters, 2021). However, social support significantly buffered these negative health symptoms, which provides insight into how allied health professionals might integrate social supports into health programs.

Applying the bioecological model to the SDOH provides a framework for understanding individuals' and communities' experiences of racism and their related health outcomes. To fully understand how racism affects health, and how allied health professionals can take antiracist action to improve health in our communities, we need to explore additional influences of racism on health, other critical issues, and current practices in the field.

Critical Issues and Practices

Physiological Effects of Racism

Racism and related discrimination can negatively affect your physiological processes in both the short and long term. Stressors such as racism and other forms of discrimination contribute to increased **allostatic load**, which can accelerate illness and aging, known as **weathering**. When individuals experience the stress of repeated discrimination, physiological changes occur in their body – specifically changes in the neurological, endocrine, and immune systems (McEwen & Stellar, 1993). Adolescents who have experienced interpersonal and systemic racial discrimination had more health-harming behaviors such as substance use, behavior problems such as conduct disorder and aggressive behavior, and negative health impacts including increased cortisol levels (Priest et al., 2013). Cortisol is sometimes known as the "stress hormone" as it helps the body regulate the stress response. Chronically elevated cortisol contributes to a variety of symptoms such as weight gain, high blood sugar, and high blood pressure (Cleveland Clinic, 2021). Over time, these negative physiological changes contribute to increased morbidity and mortality, particularly related to cardiovascular disease, diabetes, obesity, and hypertension (high blood pressure) (Miller et al., 2021). In addition, increased allostatic load is associated with depression, cognitive impairments, and poorer self-rated health. Multiple studies have demonstrated that chronic stress experienced due to racism, including childhood racism, can lead to increased allostatic load and a range of poor health outcomes (Miller et al., 2021).

Through the same series of physiological stress responses, adverse childhood experiences (ACEs) such as abuse, bullying, and parental loss are widely recognized to increase the risk of adolescent and adult physical and mental illness (Felitti et al., 1998). However, racism has not typically been included in experiences that contribute to ACEs. **Racial stress and trauma** (RST) contribute to psychological distress, high allostatic load, and reduced self-esteem and personal control, particularly for people who experience structural racism through negative SDOH (Hope et al., 2021). Subsequently, RST is a known risk factor for development of depression, particularly when individuals are (hyper) vigilant to racial discrimination (Woody et al., 2022). When youth experience racism-related threats, they process this trauma by becoming both voluntarily and involuntarily (automatically) vigilant to threat-relevant cues (Woody et al., 2022). Vigilance can be developmentally adaptive for young people, because it allows them to read interpersonal interactions and environments for potential harm, such as racism-related threats. However, adolescents who report high levels of vigilance to racism-related threats are at increased risk for RST and depression (Woody et al., 2022). This is particularly true for Black and Latine adolescents. It is imperative that health professionals consider the physical and mental health impacts of racism as they formulate their actions to promote health in those they serve.

Implicit Bias and Microaggressions in Health Care

Another racism-related issue that has gained attention in recent years is implicit bias. Implicit biases are those unconscious beliefs and attitudes that individuals, regardless of their education and socioeconomic status, hold about people by race/ethnicity. These are different, and more common in healthcare settings, than explicit bias which people may openly express and can control. Racial microaggressions can stem from both implicit and explicit bias and are frequent verbal, behavioral, or environmental indignities that convey negative, derogatory racial insults toward people of color (Sue et al., 2007). Microaggressions can appear as a microassault, microinsult, or microinvalidation. A microassault is an explicitly negative racial attack, such as using a racial epithet or prioritizing care for a White client before someone of color. Microinsults are rude and insensitive communications that demean people's racial heritage or identity. An example of a microinsult could be when a client questions a Black health professional's qualifications. Lastly, a microinvalidation negates the thoughts, feelings, or reality of a person of color (Sue et al., 2007).

Microinvalidations resulting from implicit bias can occur frequently in healthcare settings. One example is that healthcare providers may minimize the pain experienced by clients of color, because they hold an implicit bias that certain racial groups are likely to "be dramatic." This can lead to poor healthcare quality and outcomes, as health providers may not offer pain management or try to identify the root cause of the pain. Inadequate pain management not only slows healing, but not addressing the source of pain can lead to worsening illness or death. An example of this is when a Black woman's pain concerns are dismissed as they are viewed as "a strong Black woman" who can handle it (Adebayo et al., 2024). Microaggressions, racial stress and trauma, along with institutionalized racism that contribute to negative SDOH and lower healthcare quality, have led to extreme disparities in U.S. women's maternal morbidity and mortality. Black women are three to four times more likely to die from pregnancy complications compared to non-Hispanic White women of the same educational level (Adebayo et al., 2024). This is just one example of why health professionals must unite to combat racism to promote health equity and well-being for all.

Strategies for Addressing Racism

With an understanding of how systemic, interpersonal, and internalized racism can affect our clients through childhood, adolescence, and adulthood, we will explore approaches that allied health professionals can take to mitigate these effects and to promote healthy development of our clients. Antiracist strategies can be undertaken at various levels of intervention. Making change at the systemic or institutionalized levels can seem daunting and must be taken up by interprofessional teams who work in partnership with affected communities. At the interpersonal level, health professionals may find opportunities to make changes in their individual interactions with clients, such as disrupting bias and microaggressions. These interpersonal change efforts are best undertaken when colleagues, organizational structures, or policies support individual provider's efforts. Tackling internalized racism, such as the physical and mental health effects of racial stress and trauma (RST), also calls for cultivating communities who provide positive, caring peer support to one another. Thus, the bioecological model as applied to the SDOH offers a framework that simultaneously integrates multiple levels of intervention.

Developing Protective Factors

Let's start with efforts to prevent or address internalized racism. Coyne-Beasley et al. (2023) suggest cultivating a positive cultural identity and political socialization, which is also called **racial-ethnic political socialization** or RES. This positive youth development approach, which was introduced in Chapter 1, is explicitly noncolor-blind, as it cultivates protective factors such as cultural pride through group allyship and facilitated analysis of racial and other forms of discrimination. RES has been shown to prevent the internalization of racism, improve mental health, and increase **agency** (feelings of self-efficacy) and academic achievement among youth of color (Coyne-Beasley et al., 2023).

The **empower action model** includes coaching parents to cultivate RES among their children, using an intergenerational, ecological model (Srivastav et al., 2020). This empowerment framework helps promote health across the lifespan and address negative SDOH by fostering understanding, support, inclusion, connection, and growth. These collective approaches can help prevent or heal trauma by cultivating inclusive environments and protective factors within families, such cultural-racial-ethnic pride, positive relationships, and resilience (Srivastav et al., 2020). Allied health professionals can employ the empower action model to cultivate families' and communities' opportunities to collectively analyze their environments, strategize how to better cope with health stressors such as racism, and plan to create systemic change. At the same time, health professionals should recognize that racial disparities exist in health care access, treatment, and outcomes, and offer resources to families as they collectively work toward fostering environments that promote health and well-being.

While the above strategy addresses internalized racism through community-based interventions, there are similar developmental approaches that health professionals can take in their work with individual clients. One analysis of a variety of antiracist mental health practice recommendations (Miller et al., 2018) offered strategies that integrate some of the same ideas as RES and the empower action model:

- Validate racism experiences
- Offer psychoeducation: teach culturally responsive coping strategies
- Facilitate self-awareness and critical consciousness: help clients understand the intersection of race and other historically marginalized identities
- Provide culturally responsive social support: encourage the development of and connection to cultural/ethnic community and allies
- Foster the development of positive identity: explore clients' strengths and opportunities associated with multicultural experiences
- Assist with externalizing and minimizing self-blame or negative race-based messages
- Guide a critical examination of privilege and power and of racial attitudes
- Engage clients in advocacy and build agency

These individual practice recommendations mirror many of the collective approaches seen in RES and the empower action model, suggesting that there are core concepts that inform health professionals' antiracist health practices across a variety of contexts and settings. It might be helpful to see these concepts exemplified in a practical example, which is situated in a fictional high school.

Practical Example: Strategies for Addressing Racial Stress and Trauma with Adolescents

Dubois High School staff, administrators, community partners, and students have taken a collaborative approach to promoting the health, well-being, and academic success of their 1,000 students. This approach was born out of poor health and academic outcomes for their students, of whom 30% identified as Black, 25% as Latine, 20% Asian or Pacific Islander, 15% as White, and 10% as mixed race/ethnicity. The mental and physical health status of students was apparent in multiple measures, including high rates of referrals, suspensions, and expulsions for behavioral incidents and drug/alcohol use/possession, poor outcomes on physical fitness tests, and violence in the community (including the recent shooting death of a student). Results from the Dubois High School Youth Risk Behavior Survey (YRBS, 2024) indicated that a high percentage of students stated that they felt hopeless, depressed, and even suicidal, were using alcohol and drugs, were engaging in unprotected sex, had exposure to community violence, felt unsafe at school, and were consuming a low-nutrient diet. The *school nurse* and *health assistant* presented aggregated health office data reflecting some of these trends, including students frequently expressing mental health concerns, a need for sexual health care, food insecurity, and unhealthy coping including drug, alcohol, and tobacco use.

Box 5.1 Youth Risk Behavior Surveillance System

The Youth Risk Behavior Surveillance System is a national survey and reporting system conducted by the CDC to assess the health-related adolescent behaviors and experiences of American youth, including diet, sexual behavior, substance use, experiences of violence, mental health, suicidal thoughts and behaviors, bullying, and social media use. Learn more and read related YRBS reports at https://www.cdc.gov/yrbs/about/index.html

---

The *school nurse, health assistant, school social worker, guidance counselors, school psychologist, assistant principals, security officers, classroom teachers, and community partners* met with *student leaders* to collectively identify what strategies they wanted to employ to improve student health. Over several collaborative meetings, they decided to develop the following programs:

- A facilitated restorative justice circle
- Several student affinity groups organized by race/ethnicity
- An alcohol and drug treatment support group
- On-campus sexual health services, and
- Improved food, beverage, and wellness programs

The team also agreed that this ambitious set of proposed programs required a three-phase approach that would be overseen by a School Health Advisory Council (SHAC) including students, parents, school staff, and community partners.

In phase one, the SHAC held additional planning meetings facilitated by a local nonprofit *community development organization*, where they explored how racism and community environmental factors (social determinants of health) were contributing to the health challenges the students were experiencing. *Students* and *parents*, in particular, identified that their neighborhood was under-resourced: there was not a local supermarket or community health center, there was chronic under-employment in their community which seemed to contribute to local crime, and the only park in the area, just a block from the school, was seen as unsafe and did not offer any programs or equipment. In addition, members of the SHAC described how shifting neighborhood and school demographics had led to increased tensions between members of different racial/ethnic groups. The facilitators helped SHAC participants see how the emerging health issues were not the fault of individual students' poor choices or health habits; many of these health stressors were related to systemic inequities reflected in their social, economic, housing, and service contexts. Some SHAC participants, and especially students and parents, were able to identify how intergenerational racial stress and trauma contributed to some families engaging in poor coping strategies, such as drug, alcohol, and tobacco use.

Then, the SHAC members listed all the individual and community assets they could harness to best support student health needs. These strengths included resilience and adaptability in overcoming hardship, many technical and professional skills, gardening and cooking skills, community organizing skills, coaching and sports experience, graffiti arts, and connections with a variety of health service organizations in the city. The SHAC mapped identified assets to their proposed programs, and started to identify which individuals, groups, and community organizations would initiate each health program.

In phase two, the SHAC focused on developing student affinity groups and the restorative justice circles. The *school social worker* and a *guidance counselor*, with assistance from a local nonprofit, launched these groups. Their first step was to identify students who would act as *peer leaders* for each group, along with their adult ally. In consultation with school administration, they scheduled the groups to take place over lunch time, and shifted the bell schedule to allow more time for students to get their lunches and join an affinity group if interested. The school and nonprofit staff and student leaders developed a curriculum for each affinity group, which would lead participating students through a process of identifying challenges, assets, and desires just as the SHAC members had done. In addition, facilitators guided students in validating potential racism experiences, celebrating the strengths of their multicultural identities, and in developing culturally responsive support structures both inside and outside of their affinity group meetings.

The restorative justice circle operated with regularly scheduled meetings, as well as drop-in and as-needed convenings with students who had exhibited behavioral issues during the school day. Instead of being suspended, students were required to participate in at least five restorative justice circles. Students who were harmed by others participated in facilitated conversations with those who had engaged in harmful actions, to explore what happened and what justice looked like and how it could be restored. Also in phase two, a *community health promoter* trained *teachers* on how to integrate simple, brief mindfulness exercises into classes such as slow breathing and gentle movements that students could engage in to reduce their stress.

In phase three, a *psychologist* from a community mental health organization started offering on-campus alcohol, tobacco and other drug (ATOD) cessation groups. These groups were funded through Medicaid billing and local and federal substance abuse prevention grants. Instead of being suspended or expelled due to suspected ATOD use, students and their parent/guardian were required to sign a contract agreeing to participate in at least five ATOD cessation groups. A core component of the groups was helping students identify why they were using (such as stress, anxiety, or trauma), and in training them to employ more positive coping mechanisms. The ATOD groups also had young adult guest speakers who shared their stories of how they quit using ATOD.

Meanwhile, the *school nurse* and *health assistant* established an agreement such that a local community clinic *nurse practitioner* and *licensed vocational nurse* (LVN) offered services in the school health office every Monday. During this pop-up clinic, students could receive confidential services, including tests for pregnancy and sexually transmitted infections, condoms, and birth control. In addition, they offered sports physicals and vaccinations required for high school or college. These services were funded through Medicaid billing and local grants.

At the same time, a local *health educator* convened a student nutrition, fitness, and wellness action committee. This group worked with school food services staff to improve the nutritional offerings, including a lunchtime salad bar and grab-and-go sandwiches, and a free "second chance" late breakfast for students who did not have a chance to eat before school started. Student action committee members surveyed their peers regarding desired fitness activities, and then started lunchtime or afterschool intramural dance, yoga, running, and soccer programs, which were led by student and staff volunteers.

In their most ambitious, two-year undertaking, *student action committee members* and *community health workers* held three planning meetings with students, families, and staff, to develop an advocacy agenda for developing access and programming at the local park. Over 100 students and community members participated in advocacy actions with the city parks and recreation department, the city council, and the school board. They fought for and won funding and donations for equipment, improved lighting, structural improvements to the basketball court, development of a community garden, and weekday *recreation specialist* 3–7pm at their local park. High school students with graffiti arts skills created art reflecting their cultural/ethnic diversity on approved park structures and high school buildings. All participants felt increased community pride, and *students*, in particular, felt increased feelings of self-efficacy and agency as they engaged in these collaborative advocacy actions. Also, for the first time, *community elders* engaged with *high school students* and *younger children* as they led the development and stewardship of the park's community garden and cooking classes at the high school.

Practical Example Debrief

The Dubois High School example highlights the many ways that adolescents, school staff, community health workers, and families can work together. Note all the different individuals and groups (*italicized* for emphasis in the example) who were involved in different elements of their health-promoting work. Together, they were able to alleviate racial stress and trauma by developing protective factors as they facilitated restorative healing, highlighted multicultural assets, engaged in intergenerational collaboration, increased access to developmentally appropriate healthcare, and united to advocate for improved health conditions and resources in their community. While this exemplar may seem idealized, many of the related approaches have been successfully implemented by school communities.

Building Community Power

One of the core principles threaded throughout the Dubois High School example is a focus on student (client)-driven programs and advocacy. To make policy and systematic change, allied health professionals must partner with their clients to build community power, as this can contribute both directly and indirectly to improving health (Iton et al., 2022). Community power can protect health directly, such as when Black residents in Flint, Michigan organized with

Concerned Pastors for Social Action of Michigan, to sue the city and the state of Michigan over the city's failure to monitor and control lead in Flint's drinking water, which led to a plan to remove lead from residents' drinking water (Natural Resources Defense Council, 2024). Community action can also increase social support and inclusion, which can boost trust and agency within a community and improve participants' mental health (Iton et al., 2022). These concepts reinforce the utility of the empower action model (Srivastav et al., 2020) and the "racial-ethnic political socialization" positive youth development approach (Coyne-Beasley et al., 2023).

This approach builds on Popay's community empowerment model (2010) which offers pathways that link community engagement to health improvement. Iton et al. (2022) offer a new model for focusing on how building power to change health conditions within communities improves health outcomes for individuals and communities. In this model, when health professionals shift from *informing* or *consulting* communities to *collaborating with* and *deferring to* communities, there are several positive outcomes that contribute to improved health conditions. These outcomes include (1) more appropriate and accessible health services and uptake; (2) improved skills, confidence, and sense of power for individuals; (3) increased social trust, cohesion, and sense of combined power; and (4) improved community health and reduced health disparities (Iton et al., 2022). As communities engage in their collective efforts to change their health environments or systems, they may also be redressing historical and current discrimination and marginalization – which can reduce the physical and mental health effects of racial stress and trauma.

To mitigate the negative health effects of racism, funders, researchers, policymakers, and community organizations should focus on funding opportunities for community members to develop their own health advocacy agenda, rather than focusing solely on individuals' behaviors, genes, and healthcare access (Iton et al., 2022). While antiracist health professionals working in public health settings may focus on building community power to improve health, we must simultaneously attend to combating racism in healthcare settings, such as hospitals and clinics.

Disrupting Bias and Microaggressions

Instances of both explicit and implicit bias among health professionals contributed to the development of the concept of **cultural humility** (Tervalon & Murray-Garcia, 1998). Upon witnessing inadequate pain management offered to patients of color, two physicians developed this new approach for health professionals to adopt in their practice. These physicians coined the term cultural humility instead of "cultural competency" which tends to stereotype ethnic and cultural groups, and implies that health professionals' work in engaging in antiracist practice is complete once they are deemed "competent." In cultural humility, the health professional not only listens carefully to the individual symptoms and desires of each client without making assumptions, but they also engage in advocacy partnerships with their clients.

The tenets of cultural humility are:

- Nurturing a lifelong commitment to self-evaluation and self-critique.
- Redressing power imbalances in a variety of interpersonal dynamics, including the patient-clinician, client-human service professional, educator-trainee, colleague-colleague, academic center-community dynamic.
- Developing mutually beneficial and non-paternalistic clinical and advocacy partnerships with communities.
- Stewarding organizational-level developmental processes that are ongoing, and that parallel the above tenets of cultural humility (Tervalon & Murray-Garcia, 1998).

By engaging in cultural humility, health professionals can reflect on their implicit biases, and take a lifelong learning approach to understanding each individual client they serve. In this way, health professionals will not make assumptions based on stereotypes, and instead develop respectful relationships with clients. In addition, practicing cultural humility requires leading organizational change efforts to recognize and interrupt microaggressions in clinical settings.

When allied health professionals work in clinical healthcare settings, their intersectional identities offer a rich foundation from which to provide healing care for others of equally diverse backgrounds. When the healthcare workforce is more racially diverse, racial bias and microaggressions may decrease among health professionals and with clients (Khan et al., 2023). Healthcare professionals' training programs can also effectively teach health professionals in-training to identify and interrupt microaggressions (Acholonu et al., 2020). Before you decide what type of allied health professional you would like to become, you should adopt an antiracist praxis for integrating antiracist values and practices into your work.

Developing an Antiracist Health Professional Identity

Applying Antiracist Frameworks

In a speech in 2021, the Director of the Centers for Disease Control and Prevention (CDC) Dr. Rochelle P. Walensky suggested four antiracist actions that healthcare providers and health systems can take to combat racial health disparities, using the acronym REAL (Recognize, Educate, Advocate, and Listen):

1 **R**ecognize instances where structural or interpersonal racism exists in the healthcare setting and decide to take steps to combat it

2 Educate yourself, colleagues, and the institutions you work with about the specialized needs of your clients, including how racism is a barrier to better health
3 Advocate for your clients by representing their interests and sharing resources with them to access care
4 Listen to your clients to better understand their needs and desires as you support them on their journey to better health

While the audience for this speech (CDC, 2021) was a group of hematology practitioners, the recommended actions can be applied by allied health professionals working in a variety of roles. With your deep understanding of racial disparities, biases, and microaggressions, you are now well-poised to identify when structural or interpersonal racism is at play in your healthcare setting, and to take action to disrupt racism. Employing cultural humility, you can continue to honestly examine when and how racism is affecting the health of the clients or communities you serve and advocate for change in your organization and with clients.

Here are some concrete approaches and some guiding questions for taking antiracist approaches in your practice as an allied health professional:

- **Investigate your health organization's policies and practices**: Do they support the health and well-being of employees and clients? For example, has the organization adopted bias reporting mechanisms and related tools, which can reduce discriminatory treatment? (Khan et al., 2023)
- **Explore health contexts, assets, and desires:** Are there environmental, structural, and/or service assets or barriers to health? Remember, this assessment must be done in partnership with community members. Ultimately, you may be able to identify and engage supportive resources and services that clients may not yet have access to.
- **Analyze individual client and community contexts**: Take time to explore an individual's or community's SDOH. This can be done in a variety of ways, for example conducting health assessments and key informant interviews.
- **Identify current or historical racist policies underlying identified barriers:** For example, consider historical redlining in the neighborhood, immigration policies, and economic divestment in communities of color.
- **Partner with allies:** Find like-minded health professionals who can serve as mentors or allies in your collaborative antiracist efforts, as none of us can prevent racism alone. Join health professional affinity groups, such as the National Association of Hispanic Nurses. Engage in networking opportunities that connect you with other antiracist professionals. Partner with your client communities to foster collective action to improve health conditions and environments.

Reflect and Practice Activities

Case Study Analysis: Addressing Black Perinatal and Maternal Health Disparities

Read the case study below about how one organization is working to reduce perinatal and maternal health disparities among Black women. The organization featured in the case study is fictional, but based on the programs and services in similar organizations. As you read the case study, take note of the approaches the organization's staff and other partners took to address racism. After reading the case study, you will analyze the organization's strategies with guiding reflection questions.

Background

Black Women Together's mission is to improve pregnancy, birth, and postpartum experiences for African American women in the greater metro area, as well as to reduce infant mortality rates. The core program includes pregnancy peer support, doula, health education, and lactation services to African American women. Program staff also provide individualized care plans that include personalized referrals to midwives and obstetricians in the area who take a range of private insurance and Medicaid, and who share in Black Women Together (BWT)'s values. These values center culturally sensitive care, focused on respecting and understanding the cultural background and unique experiences of African American women. Another key value is creating an inclusive environment that involves families, strengthens bonds, and enhances each woman's support networks. All BWT staff are trained in understanding the unique stressors Black mothers face, as well as in strategies to counteract the ways internalized, interpersonal, and systemic racism may contribute to maternal morbidity and mortality, such as trauma-informed care. BWT is funded through a combination of federal, state, and local grants, billing revenues, and donations. Below are the seven primary programs that BWT offers to African American women.

Peer Support Services

Each Black Women Together (BWT) client is assigned a Pregnancy Coach who develops personalized care plans for each woman. This includes helping each woman develop her plans for her pregnancy, birth, and postpartum care. The pregnancy coach helps women plan their birth experience, whether they plan to give birth at home, in a birthing center, or in a traditional hospital setting.

Access to Care

BWT enrollment workers consider what health systems each client can access with her specific insurance, and if she is uninsured, they help her enroll in Medicaid. Then, the enrollment worker helps each client schedule her prenatal appointments, her delivery, and postpartum appointments.

Prenatal and Postpartum Education

BWT provides educational programs that specifically address the needs of Black mothers, emphasizing prenatal and postpartum health, nutrition and exercise, mental health, and how to manage pregnancy-related conditions. Health Educators also carefully listen for and integrate the narratives that reflect each woman's experiences, and help to build the woman and her family's practical skills in self-advocacy in healthcare settings. The educational sessions are delivered in individual and group settings and can integrate family members if the woman prefers it.

Support Groups

BWT facilitates regular support groups with clients. From the time a pregnant woman enrolls in the program, she can join a support group that meets twice a month. The support groups provide a safe space for African American women to share their experiences, advice, and emotional support with one another. The facilitators are Health Advocates who are culturally aware and trained in normalizing (and not stigmatizing) racism-related anxiety, stressors, and trauma that women may experience. Facilitators work to provide emotional support and help mothers build an ongoing peer support network that may mitigate feelings of isolation and anxiety stemming from systemic biases.

Culturally Congruent Doulas

African American Doulas support clients' labor by offering comfort measures and advocating for birthing women with other health care providers during the delivery. Doula guidance and support in perinatal care is associated with reduced cesarean sections, premature deliveries, length of labor, and anxiety and stress (Sobczak et al., 2023). BWT is able to recruit, train, and pay for doulas through a grant from the U.S. Department of Health and Human Services intended to address the nation's Black maternal health crisis.

Lactation Support

BWT offers lactation support and education, including tips and techniques for successful breastfeeding and ways to overcome common challenges. Lactation Consultants and Doulas offer home visits to clients in the first two weeks after birth, where they can support women in the comfort of their own home. Doula or lactation consultant support in the postpartum period improves breastfeeding success and duration (Sobczak et al., 2023), which can improve infants' health.

Access to Pregnancy and Birth Supplies

BWT provides free access to essential pregnancy and birth supplies, such as prenatal vitamins, breastfeeding supplies, and a first month's supply of diapers. In addition, they partner with a program that provides free car seats for those first-time mothers who need them, including demonstrating how to correctly install the car seat.

Training and Partnership with other Maternal Health Providers

In addition to their programs for women who are pregnant and postpartum, BWT staff is trying to expand their reach into the region's health system by offering training to the healthcare providers they partner with. These training sessions include understanding African American women's historical and contemporary experiences of racial trauma, antiracist and trauma-informed care, identifying and counteracting implicit biases, and centering and listening to African American's women's birth experiences. This training allows BWT staff to trust the providers they will refer their clients to, and helps improve interactions between providers and African American women throughout the perinatal period.

Discussion Questions:

- How do Black Women Together's services improve access to and the quality of perinatal services for African American women?
- How does BWT's work employ the *community cultural wealth* model (Yosso, 2005) identified in Chapter 1, to navigate and resist racism?
- Which of BWT's approaches might help African American women counteract stress reactions and potential internalized racism?
- How do Black Women Together's services and networks try to address personally mediated (interpersonal) racism?
- Do you think that BWT is addressing systemic racism? Why or why not?
- What are some of the allied health professional roles employed by or collaborating with Black Women Together?

Interview Activity

Conduct a key informant interview with one or more community member/s regarding a specific health issue of interest. Questions may include:

- What do you believe is causing this health issue?
- What is the change or outcome you want to see?

- What solutions or approaches have been tried?
- Who has engaged in helping address this health issue?
- What community/program assets have been brought to address this issue?
- What do you think are the next step/s for community members? What actions can allied health professionals take?

Critical Questions

The reflection and discussion prompts below encourage your critical thinking and engagement with the chapter's content. In response to the prompts below, you can free-write rapid reactions, write longer papers supported by related literature, and/or formulate strategies through small group discussion in class.

1 Name three ways you can model cultural humility as a health professional, and how this may help improve quality of care and health outcomes.
2 Describe how the social determinants of health (SDOH) can influence individual or community health outcomes, and why health professionals should care about the SDOH.
3 Identify one way racism can contribute to an individual's stress and describe how that can affect health outcomes.
4 Provide an example of how health professionals can prevent racial health disparities.
5 Explain how health professionals can take an antiracist approach to community health advocacy.

Other Activity Ideas

Identify an adult health client or individual (could be a classmate, friend, or family member) you know, and in conversation with them, map out their current SDOH. Be sure to identify both assets and challenges in their home, work, school, and neighborhood environments, their economic stability, health care access and quality, and other social or community contexts.

Chapter Summary

- Systemic, interpersonal, and internalized racism presents barriers to good physical and mental health.
- Racial health disparities reflect how racism contributes to preventable differences in health outcomes.
- Health is influenced by nonmedical, environmental and structural factors called the social determinants of health.
- Individuals' stress responses to racism can negatively impact their physiological processes, leading to poor physical and mental health outcomes, such as heart disease, diabetes, and depression.

- Racism may occur in healthcare settings through the expression of implicit and explicit biases and microaggressions.
- Health professionals can adopt a variety of antiracist strategies, such as developing protective factors in youth, building community power, and disrupting microaggressions.
- Adopting a position of cultural humility and exploring implicit biases can support reflective practice and ongoing learning.
- Allied health professionals can only dismantle racism in healthcare and stop racial health disparities by partnering with colleagues and affected communities.

Recommended Resources

The following books, articles, and other resources may help you deepen your understanding of antiracism in allied health professional contexts.

- Centers for Disease Control and Prevention. (January 17, 2024). *Social determinants of health.* https://www.cdc.gov/about/priorities/why-is-addressing-sdoh-important.html
- Cooke-Jackson, A. (Ed.). (2024). Emergent health communication scholarship from and about African American, Latino/a/x, and American Indian/Alaskan Native Peoples (1st ed.). Routledge. https://doi.org/10.4324/9781032661285
- EdX. (August 2021). Anti-racism resources for students and professionals in healthcare. Nursing License Map. https://nursinglicensemap.com/resources/anti-racism-in-healthcare/
- Iton, A., Ross, R. K., & Tamber, P. S. (2022). Building community power to dismantle policy-based structural inequity in population health. *Health Affairs, 41*(12), 1763–1771. https://doi.org/10.1377/hlthaff.2022.00540.
  - Also, see the Appendix for this article: A new model linking community engagement, health improvement, and community power. https://www.healthaffairs.org/doi/suppl/10.1377/hlthaff.2022.00540/suppl_file/2022-00540_suppl_appendix.pdf
- Robert Wood Johnson Foundation. (2001–2024). *Life expectancy: Could where you live influence how long you live?* https://www.rwjf.org/en/insights/our-research/interactives/whereyouliveaffectshowlongyoulive.html

References

Aaronson, D., Hartley, D., Mazumder, B., & Stinson, M. (2023). The long-run effects of the 1930s redlining maps on children. *Journal of Economic Literature, 61*(3), 846–862. https://doi.org/10.1257/jel.20221702

Acholonu, R. G., Cook, T. E., Roswell, R. O., & Greene, R. E. (2020). Interrupting microaggressions in health care settings: A guide for teaching medical students. *MedEdPORTAL, 16*, 10969. https://doi.org/10.15766/mep_2374-8265.10969

Adebayo, C. T., Parcell, E. S., Mkandawire-Valhmu, L., & Olukotun, O. (2024). African American women's maternal healthcare experiences: A critical race theory perspective. In A. Cooke-Jackson (Ed.), *Emergent health communication scholarship from and about African American, Latino/a/x, and American Indian/Alaskan native peoples* (pp. 79–90). Routledge.

Bronfenbrenner, U., & Morris, P. (2006). The bioecological model of human development. In R. M. Lerner & W. Damon (Eds.), *Handbook of child psychology: Vol. 1. Theoretical models of human development* (6th ed., pp. 793–828). Wiley.

Centers for Disease Control and Prevention. (December 11, 2021). *Addressing health disparities and racism: Real steps toward change*. Archived 1/11/24: https://archive.cdc.gov/www_cdc_gov/ncbddd/sicklecell/addressing-health-disparities.html

Centers for Disease Control and Prevention. (January 17, 2024). *Social determinants of health*. https://www.cdc.gov/about/priorities/why-is-addressing-sdoh-important.html

Centers for Disease Control and Prevention. (June 14, 2024). *Youth risk behavior surveillance system: About YRBSS*. https://www.cdc.gov/yrbs/about/index.html

Cleveland Clinic. (December 10, 2021). *Cortisol*. https://my.clevelandclinic.org/health/articles/22187-cortisol

Conzelmann, C., Salazar Miranda, A., Phan, T., & Hoffman, J. (2022). Long-term effects of redlining on environmental risk exposure. *Federal Reserve Bank of Richmond Working Paper, 22*(9), 1–20.

Coyne-Beasley, T., Hill, S. V., Miller, E., & Svetaz, M. V. (2023). Health equity and the impact of racism on adolescent health. *Pediatrics, 151*(Supplement 1), S1–6. https://doi.org/10.1542/peds.2022-057267F

Duong, K. N. C., Le, L. M., Veettil, S. K., Saidoung, P., Wannaadisai, W., Nelson, R. E., Friedrichs, M., Jones, B. E., Pavia, A. T., Jones, M. M., Samore, M. H., & Chaiyakunapruk, N. (2023). Disparities in COVID-19 related outcomes in the United States by race and ethnicity pre-vaccination era: An umbrella review of meta-analyses. *Frontiers in Public Health, 11*(1206988), 1–9. https://doi.org/10.3389/fpubh.2023.1206988

Felitti, V. J., Anda, R. F., Nordenberg, D., Williamson, D. F., Spitz, A. M., Edwards, V., & Marks, J. S. (1998). Relationship of childhood abuse and household dysfunction to many of the leading causes of death in adults: The Adverse Childhood Experiences (ACE) Study. *American Journal of Preventive Medicine, 14*(4), 245–258. https://doi.org/10.1016/S0749-3797(98)00017-8

Hill, L., & Artiga, S. (August 22, 2022). *COVID-19 cases and deaths by race/ethnicity: Current data and changes over time*. Kaiser Family Foundation. https://www.kff.org/racial-equity-and-health-policy/issue-brief/covid-19-cases-and-deaths-by-race-ethnicity-current-data-and-changes-over-time/

Hope, E. C., Brinkman, M., Hoggard, L. S., Stokes, M. N., Hatton, V., Volpe, V. V., & Elliot, E. (2021). Black adolescents' anticipatory stress responses to multilevel racism: The role of racial identity. *American Journal of Orthopsychiatry, 91*(4), 487–498. https://doi.org/10.1037/ort0000547

Horne, G., Gautam, A., & Tumin, D. (2022). Short- and long-term health consequences of gaps in health insurance coverage among young adults. *Population Health Management, 25*(3), 399–406. https://doi.org/10.1089/pop.2021.0211

Iton, A., Ross, R. K., & Tamber, P. S. (2022). Building community power to dismantle policy-based structural inequity in population health. *Health Affairs, 41*(12), 1763–1771. https://doi.org/10.1377/hlthaff.2022.00540

Jones, C. P. (2000). Levels of racism: A theoretic framework and a gardener's tale. *American Journal of Public Health, 90*(8), 1212–1215. https://doi.org/10.2105/ajph.90.8.1212

Khan, N., Hafeez, D., Goolamallee, T., Arora, A., Smith, W., Shankar, R., & Dave, S. (2023). Racial microaggressions in healthcare settings: A scoping review. *BJPsych Open, 9*(S1), S7–S8. https://doi.org/10.1192/bjo.2023.97

Lee, S., & Waters, S. F. (2021). Asians and Asian Americans' experiences of racial discrimination during the COVID-19 pandemic: Impacts on health outcomes and the buffering role of social support. *Stigma and Health, 6*(1), 70. https://dx.doi.org/10.1037/sah0000275

McEwen, B. S., & Stellar, E. (1993). Stress and the individual: Mechanisms leading to disease. *Archives of Internal Medicine, 153*(18), 2093–2101. https://doi.org/10.1001/archinte.1993.00410180039004

Miller, M. J., Keum, B. T., Thai, C. J., Lu, Y., Truong, N. N., Huh, G. A., ... & Ahn, L. H. (2018). Practice recommendations for addressing racism: A content analysis of the counseling psychology literature. *Journal of Counseling Psychology, 65*(6), 669–680. https://dx.doi.org/10.1037/cou0000306

Miller, H. N., LaFave, S., Marineau, L., Stephens, J., & Thorpe, R. J. (2021). The impact of discrimination on allostatic load in adults: An integrative review of literature. *Journal of Psychosomatic Research, 146*(110434), 1–11. https://doi.org/10.1016/j.jpsychores.2021.110434

Natural Resources Defense Council. (May 31, 2024). Concerned pastors for social action v. Khouri. https://www.nrdc.org/court-battles/concerned-pastors-social-action-v-khouri#:~:text=In%20January%202016%2C%20NRDC%2C%20Concerned,officials%20to%20dismiss%20the%20lawsuit

Popay, J. (2010). Community empowerment and health improvement: The English experience. In A. Morgan, M. Davies & E. Ziglio (Eds.), *Health assets in a global context* (pp. 183–195). Springer. https://doi.org/10.1007/978-1-4419-5921-8_10

Priest, N., Paradies, Y., Trenerry, B., Truong, M., Karlsen, S., & Kelly, Y. (2013). A systematic review of studies examining the relationship between reported racism and health and the wellbeing for children and young people. *Social Science & Medicine, 95*, 115–127. https://doi.org/10.1016/j.socscimed.2012.11.031

Robert Wood Johnson Foundation. (2001–2024). *Life expectancy: Could where you live influence how long you live?* https://www.rwjf.org/en/insights/our-research/interactives/whereyouliveaffectshowlongyoulive.html

Rothstein, R. (2017). *The color of law: A forgotten history of how our government segregated America.* Liveright Publishing.

Ruiz, N. G., Im, C., & Tian, Z. (November 30, 2023). *Asian Americans and discrimination during the COVID-19 pandemic.* Pew Research Center Report. https://www.pewresearch.org/2023/11/30/asian-americans-and-discrimination-during-the-covid-19-pandemic/

Singh, G. K., Daus, G. P., Allender, M., Ramey, C. T., Martin, E. K., Perry, C., Reyes, A. A. L., & Vedamuthu, I. P. (2017). Social determinants of health in the United States: Addressing major health inequality trends for the nation, 1935–2016. *International Journal of Maternal Child Health and AIDS, 6*(2), 139–164. https://doi.org/10.21106/ijma.236

Smedley, B. D., Stith, A. Y., & Nelson, A. R. (Eds.). (2003). *Unequal treatment: Confronting racial and ethnic disparities in health care.* National Academy of Sciences. National Academies Press.

Sobczak, A., Taylor, L., Solomon, S., Ho, J., Phillips, B., Jacobson, K., ... & Jacobs, R. J. (2023). The effect of doulas on maternal and birth outcomes: A scoping review. *Cureus, 15*(5), e39451, 1–14. https://doi.org/10.7759/cureus.39451

Srivastav, A., Strompolis, M., Moseley, A., & Daniels, K. (2020). The empower action model: A framework for preventing adverse childhood experiences by promoting health, equity, and well-being across the life span. *Health Promotion Practice, 21*(4), 525–534. https://doi.org/10.1177/1524839919889355

Sue, D. W., Capodilupo, C. M., Torino, G. C., Bucceri, J. M., Holder, A. M. B., Nadal, K. L., & Esquilin, M. (2007). Racial microaggressions in everyday life: Implications for clinical practice. *American Psychologist, 62*(4), 271–286. https://doi.org/10.1037/0003-066X.62.4.271

Swope, C. B., Hernández, D., & Cushing, L. J. (2022). The relationship of historical redlining with present-day neighborhood environmental and health outcomes: A scoping review and conceptual model. *Journal of Urban Health, 99*(6), 959–983. https://doi.org/10.1007/s11524-022-00665-z

Tervalon, M., & Murray-Garcia, J. (1998) Cultural humility versus cultural competence: A critical distinction in defining physician training outcomes in multicultural education. *Journal of Health Care for the Poor and Underserved, 9*(2), 117–125. https://doi.org/10.1353/hpu.2010.0233

Woody, M. L., Bell, E. C., Cruz, N. A., Wears, A., Anderson, R. E., & Price, R. B. (2022). Racial stress and trauma and the development of adolescent depression: A review of the role of vigilance evoked by racism-related threat. *Chronic Stress, 6*, 1–13. https://doi.org/10.1177/24705470221118574

Yosso, T. J. (2005). Whose culture has capital? A critical race theory discussion of community cultural wealth. *Race Ethnicity and Education, 8*(1), 69–91. https://doi.org/10.1080/1361332052000341006

Index

Note: *Italic* page numbers refer to figures.

ACEs *see* adverse childhood experiences (ACEs)
"achievement gap" 71, 100
adolescents: child and 4–6, 8, 10, 27, 33, 34, 60, 88, 100, 117, 118; risk of 119; RST with 122–125; uninsured and underinsured ages 113
adverse childhood experiences (ACEs) 119
advocacy 127, 130; engaging in 97; for marginalized groups 18; student (client)-driven programs and 125
Advocates for Equity in Education (AEE) 106
affinity groups 123, 124, 128
African American Doulas 130
African American Vernacular English (AAVE) 67
African American women 129–131
agency 5, 38, 121; for collective advocacy 115; self-efficacy and 125; sense of 80, 94–96, 99; trust and 126
Alaska Native Cultural Identity Project 41–42
alcohol, tobacco and other drug (ATOD) cessation groups 124
Alexander, M. 46
alignment of structural diversity 91
allied health professionals 27, 113–115; antiracist health professional identity 127–128; health disparities 115; implicit bias and microaggressions 119–120; physiological effects of racism 118–119; reflect and practice activities 129–132; SDOH 115–118; strategies for addressing racism 120–127

allostatic load 114, 118, 119
American Psychological Association (APA) 32, 53
antiracism/antiracist 6, 9; aligning with principles 93; allied health professionals *see* allied health professionals; antiracist development frameworks *see* antiracist development frameworks; audit of psychological concepts and measures 50–52; developmental view of higher education *see* antiracist developmental view, of higher education; educational context 74; frameworks 103–104; health professionals 126–128; lens 18–21, 37, 68; practices 6, 83; praxis interview 108–109; principles in practice 97; professional 16–18; professional identity, within psychology *see* antiracist professional identity, within psychology; within psychology 49–50; strategies 26, 120; teacher 62; teaching development, in PK-12 education *see* antiracist developmental teaching, in PK-12 education; *see also* racism/racial
antiracist cultural responsive classroom management 72–74
antiracist developmental teaching, in PK-12 education 26–27, 58–60; case study analysis 80–82; critical reflective practice 68–72; "culturally responsive" classroom management 72–74; foundations of teacher identity 60–63; frameworks 72–76; opportunities for developing critical literacy 75–76;

practical example 76–80; practices in education 83; restorative practices 74; teachers 62–63; traditional educational goals 74–75; Vygotsky's ZPD 63–65, *64*; WZPD 65–67, *66*
antiracist developmental view, of higher education 27, 87–89, 95–96; advocacy 97; affirming and sustaining student identity 92–93; centering relationships and emotional support 96–97; critical issues and considerations 99–104; intersectionality and critical consciousness in student development 93–95; mentorship and support systems 97–99; MMDLE 89–92; professional identity 104–105; reflect and practice activities 105–109
antiracist development frameworks 4–6, 10–17; definitions 7–10; professional 17–26
antiracist developmental science 5, 59
Antiracist Praxis Model 2, 17, 22–24, 80, 81, 102–105; in professional life 25; sustainable antiracist practice 26
antiracist professional identity: community psychology 48–49; critical psychology 45–46; liberation psychology 46–48
APA *see* American Psychological Association (APA)
aspirational capital 13
assessments: campus climate 101–102; formative assessment, ZPD 65; psychological measures and 39–41
asset-based community development 49
ATOD cessation groups *see* alcohol, tobacco and other drug (ATOD) cessation groups
avoiding euphemisms 69

behavior chart 74, 76–79
BHC *see* Black Honors College (BHC)
biases 12, 68, 96; and impact on development 100; and microaggressions 126–127
bioecological model 10–13, *11*, 16, 33, 48, 103; Bronfenbrenner's 88–89; SDOH and 116–118, 120
Black: adults 14; health professional 120; and Latine communities 116; perinatal and maternal health disparities 129–131; student 67; woman 120

Black Honors College (BHC) 102–103
Black-Serving Institution (BSI) 102–104
Black Success Initiative 103
Black Women Together (BWT) 129–131
brainstorm longer-term strategies 107
Brodsky, A. E. 36
Bronfenbrenner, U. 59; bioecological systems model 27, 88–90, 116; mesosystem 90
Buckingham, S. L. 42
building power, within communities 115, 126
Burman, E. 45
BWT *see* Black Women Together (BWT)

California State University (CSU) system 102
campus climate: assessments 101–102; equity audit 108; and organizational practices (MMDLE) 90, 92
Cattaneo, L. B. 36
"Caucasian" 8
"celebrating diverse cultural traditions" 73
centering relationships, in higher education 96–97
challenge societal inequities 60
challenge systemic racism 59; *see also* racism/racial
Chamberlain, K. 46
Chavez, C. 76
chronosystem: bioecological model *11*; MMDLE 89; SDOH 118
civic engagement 74
classroom environment 78; curriculum choices and representation 78–79; management and equity literacy 60, 79–80; norms 71; teacher positionality and racial literacy 79
classroom management system 75
coded language 69, 71–72, 83
collaborating with and deferring to communities 126
collaborative learning 64, 65
collaborative learning activities 64
colorblind racism 8, 17; *see also* racism/racial
colorblind racism approaches 70
community: agreements 74; cultural wealth model 13, 14; development organization 123; engagement 43; health promoter 124; health workers 125; impacted communities 43–45;

inclusion and partnership 49; and organizing capacity-building 49; power 44, 125–126, 133; program development and management 49; psychology 45, 48–49; readiness 82, 107; research 49; resilience 95–96; and social change 49
community-based participatory research 44
community-engaged research 44
community psychology 45, 48–49
Community Tool Box 50, 53
Concerned Pastors for Social Action of Michigan 126
connecting theory-to-practice 5
context, role of bioecological model 10–12
contextualized role of a teacher 59
continuous professional development 68
cooperative learning groups 73
cortisol 119
counseling psychology programs 45
COVID-19 pandemic 100, 115, 118
Coyne-Beasley, T. 121
Crenshaw, K. 9, 94
critical: consciousness *see* critical consciousness; literacy 73–76; psychology 45–46; reflection 15, 22, 25, 37, 45, 59, 68, 72
critical consciousness 17, 37–38, 58; in student development 93–95; in teachers 66–67
critical reflection 15, 22, 25, 37, 45, 59, 68, 72, 94
critical reflective practice 60, 67–72
cultivating protective factors 115
cultural/ethnic community and allies 121
"culturally responsive" classroom management 72–74
culturally responsive coping strategies 121
culturally sustaining pedagogy 78
cultural-racial-ethnic pride 121
culture/cultural: awareness 68; beliefs 35; capital 13–14; competency 126; educational buzzwords 73; humility 32, 35, 114, 126–128, 132, 133; "normalized" values of racism 117; perspective-taking 74; and policy-driven macrosystem 89; socialization 12
curriculum choices and representation 60, 78–79

decenter Whiteness 79
deficit perspective 79, 99
developing equity literacy 70, 75–76
development/developmental: antiracist perspectives, on Pre-K-12 teaching 58; context of socialization 61; and educational psychology 63; psychology 100; racial literacy 61; theories 59, 103
developmentally appropriate healthcare 125
developmentally informed mentorship and support systems 97–99
DFW rate 101
discipline disparity 26
differentiated instruction 64, 65
dismantle racism 5, 133; *see also* racism/racial
disrupting microaggressions 114–115, 133
"diverse" 8, 14, 18, 20, 39, 40, 71, 73, 74, 76, 87–93, 95, 98, 101, 105, 106, 108, 127
diversity: "heroes and holidays" representations of 78; tax 98
dominant cultural perspectives 73
Dubois High School Youth Risk Behavior Survey 122, 125

early-career professionals 97; in child and adolescent development 4; students and 1
Early Career Steps for Developing an Antiracist Lens in Your Profession 2, 5, 17–22, 68
ecocultural theory 26, 34–35, 38
ecological: analysis 81, 106–107; model 10, *11*, 88–89; perspectives 14, 48, 49; systems 68; theories 10, 48
education/educational systems 68; antiracist practices in 83; ecosystem 91; lactation support and 130–131; prenatal and postpartum 130; ZPD in 65; *see also* higher education
egalitarianism 12
embracing antiracist practices 6
emotional labor 98
empower action model 121–122, 126
empowerment 26, 35–37, 42, 47–50, 121
engaging in advocacy 97
engaging with diverse stakeholders 68
environmental indignities 119–120
equity audit 105, 108

equity literacy: classroom management and 79–80; racial and 72, 77, 82, 83; for teachers 70–71
Erikson, E. 59
ethical, reflective practice 49
ethnic-racial socialization 11–12
Ethnic Studies 92
ethnotheories 26, 34–35, 38
examining curricular materials 70
exclusionary discipline, consequences of 80–82
exosystem 35; bioecological model 11, *11*; MMDLE 89; SDOH 117
extensive research 98

familial capital 14
Ferreira van Leer, K. 92, 93
first generation students 99
formative assessment 65; *see also* assessments
fostering critical consciousness 17, 94; *see also* critical consciousness
foundations/foundational: awareness 68; of teacher identity 60–63; theories 59
Fox, D. 46
Freire, P. 17, 37, 42, 44
function as complex ecosystems 87

Garcia, G. A. 93
Gough, B. 45
grading policies 105–107; *see also* policies
grading practices 106
"grit" 76, 79
"growth mindset" 76, 79
guided practice 25
Gulley, N. Y. 92

healing justice 38, 41–42
health: disparities 39, 114, 115, 126, 127, 129, 132; educators 124, 130; professionals 113; service delivery 114; White racial identity development 70
health care: implicit bias and microaggressions in 119–120; professionals' training programs 127
hematology practitioners 128
Henrich, J. 38
Hergenrather, K. C. 44
higher education: affirming and sustaining student identity in 92–93; antiracist developmental view of

see antiracist developmental view, of higher education; bioecological lens 87; centering relationships and emotional support 96–97; ecological model for 88–89; racial and cultural dynamics in 90; racial justice 88; REM (Racially and Ethnically Marginalized) communities in 100; *see also* education/educational systems
Hispanic-Serving Institutions (HSIs) 92
holidays and heroes 72, 78
holistic support 103
HSIs *see* Hispanic-Serving Institutions (HSIs)
Hurtado, S. 90, 91

identify inequity(ies) 23
Identify supportive resources 24, 82, 107
immediate and long-term personal action steps 24, 82, 107
impacted communities 43–45; *see also* community
implicit bias and microaggressions in healthcare 119–120
imposter syndrome 96, 99, 109
inclusive school policies 71–72; *see also* policies
individual/interpersonal level 60, 113, 120
individualism 66
individual meaning-making 15–16
inequities 45, 46, 105–106; challenge societal inequities 60; within classroom 71–72; educational inequities 69, 115; exacerbated inequities 43; health 113; institutional 27; issues of 26; perpetuate inequities 50, 62; in policies 22; by race and perpetuating racism 32; racial 9, 38, 39; social 15; structural inequities 37, 68, 69, 100; systemic inequities 8, 18, 19, 21, 61, 73, 74, 79, 90, 123
informed mentorship and support systems 97–99
institutional context (MMDLE) 90, 91, 100, 102, 104
institutionalized racism 9, 120; *see also* racism/racial
Integrative Model *see* Integrative Model of Ethnic Minority Development
Integrative Model of Ethnic Minority Development 14–16
Intellectual humility 18

interconnected contexts (MMDLE) 88, 90
interconnected principles 2
internalization 9, 64–65, 121
internalized racism 9, 27, 120, 121, 131; see also racism/racial
interpersonal and systemic racial discrimination 118–119
intersectionality 9, 19, 27, 28, 96, 103, 104; in student development 93–95
interwoven systems, of privilege and oppression 94
Iruka, I. U. 100
Iton, A. 126

Jones, C. P. 8
justice-centered perspective, on human development 2

Kelly, J. 48
Kendi, I. X. 9
Khuankaew, O. 47
King, M. L. Jr. 76

Lactation Consultants and Doulas 130–131
lactation support 130–131
Lareau, A. 34
leadership programs, with social justice lens 94–95
learning: antiracist strategies 114; collaborative 64; cooperative learning groups 73; facilitators of 63; mediate 63; project-based 64; Universal Design 77
Leonardo, Z. 65, 66
Lewin, K. 44
liberation and counseling psychology 47–48
liberation psychology 45–47, 53
licensed vocational nurse (LVN) 124
lifelong learning approach 127
'like-with-like' approach 98
linguistic capital 14
LVN see licensed vocational nurse (LVN)

macrosystem: bioecological model 11, *11*; MMDLE 89; SDOH 117–118
Manning, L. 65, 66
mapping systems 109
Martín-Baró, I. 44, 46
maternal health disparities 129–131
McKay, S. 44
McWayne, C. M. 35, 41

mentors/mentorship 15, 18, 49, 91, 104, 108, 128; BHC and 104; and professional networks 20–21, 68; reflective practice for 98; and support systems 97–99
mesosystem: bioecological model 11, *11*; MMDLE 89, 90; SDOH 117
microaggressions 100; bias and 126–127; in health care 119–120
microassault 120
microinsults 120
microinvalidations 120
microsystem 34, 35; bioecological model 11, *11*; MMDLE 89–92; SDOH 117
microsystem and student interactions (MMDLE) 90–91
mistrust 12, 44
MKO see More Knowledgeable Other (MKO)
MMDLE see Multicontextual Model for Diverse Learning Environments (MMDLE)
Montero, M. 43
More Knowledgeable Other (MKO) 64
Multicontextual Model for Diverse Learning Environments (MMDLE) 27, 88–89, 108; and Antiracist Praxis Model 106; Bronfenbrenner's foundational bioecological model 89–90; components of 90–91; understanding and applying 91–92
multidimensional system of oppression and exclusion 4
multilayered outcomes (MMDLE) 91
multiple SDOH 118

National Association of Hispanic Nurses 128
National Institutes of Health and the National Science Foundation 39
navigating and resisting a racist system 98–99
navigational capital 13, 98
negative effects, of systemic racism 14
negative race-based messages 121
neighborhood collective efficacy 14
"9/11" World Trade Center bombing 117
Norsworthy, K. L. 47

Ogunyemi, D. 100
one-size-fits-all approach 78
ongoing reflective practices 98
"opportunity gap" 67, 71

Parental Engagement of Families from Latine backgrounds (PELF) 40
participatory action research 44
partnering directly with impacted communities 43–45
peer leaders 123
peer-led activities 95
peer support services 129
PELF *see* Parental Engagement of Families from Latine backgrounds (PELF)
personal biases 17, 20, 108
personally-mediated racism 8–9; *see also* racism/racial
person, role of bioecological model 10–11
perspective exploration 23, 81, 106
Phenomenological Variant of Ecological Systems Theory (PVEST) 15–16, 33
physiological stress responses 119
physiological weathering 114, 118
Piaget, J. 59
PK-12 contexts, antiracist developmental frameworks in: "culturally responsive" classroom management 72–74; opportunities for developing critical literacy 75–76; restorative practices 74; traditional educational goals 74–75
PK-12 education: antiracist developmental teaching in 26–27 *see also* antiracist developmental teaching, in PK-12 education; teaching 63
policies: grading 105–107; inclusive school 70–71; inequities in 22; MMDLE 102–103; racist policies 114; school 60, 61, 70–71, 73
Popay, J.: community empowerment model (2010) 126
positionality 62, 66, 94, 98; personal biases and 108; shapes 59; social positionality 18; teacher 27, 79
positive intergroup interactions 91
"post-traditional" students 87, 105, 106
praxis 32, 37, 127
pregnancy and birth supplies 131
prenatal and postpartum education 130
prevention programs 48
problematization 38, 42–43, 46, 47, 53
process-person-context-time 13
project-based learning 64, 73, 75
protective factors 14, 121–125, 133; for positive youth development 15

physiological effects of racism 27, 115, 118–119
psychological research 38–39; and practitioners 39–41
psychology: antiracist professional identity within *see* antiracist professional identity, within psychology; community 48–49; counseling programs 45; critical 45–46; developmental psychology 100; liberation 46–47; Liberation and Counseling Psychology 47–48; racism through *see* racism, through psychology
purposeful action 25
PVEST *see* Phenomenological Variant of Ecological Systems Theory (PVEST)

race 7–8, 12–14, 17–21, 26, 32, 35, 39, 40, 44, 51, 59, 61–63, 65, 67–70, 83, 93, 94, 98, 103, 114, 119, 121–123
race-evasive 73, 83
racelighting 96, 99, 108
race-neutral 8, 58
racial equity 7, 8, 60
racial-ethnic political socialization (RES) 121–122; positive youth development approach 126
racial literacy 8, 77; teacher positionality and 79; for teachers 69–70
"racial macro stressor" 100
racial mediation 66
racial stress and trauma (RST) 119, 120, 122–126
racism/racial: and anti-Islamic attitudes 118; building community power 125–126; challenge systemic racism 59; colorblind racism 8, 70; and cultural dynamics, in higher education 90; developing protective factors 121–125; development and 10–17; dismantle racism 5; disparities, in health outcomes 114; disrupting bias and microaggressions 126–127; and equity literacies 7, 68; health disparities 115, 127; identity 72; impacts of 14; institutionalized racism 9, 120; internalized racism 9, 120, 121; justice 88; literacy *see* racial literacy; mediation, WZPD framework 66;

microaggressions 119–120; navigating and resisting 98–99; perpetuate racism 5; personallymediated racism 8–9; physiological effects of 118–119; process-person-context-time to 13; and racist policies 114; related threats 119; and SDOH 115–116; structural racism 9; systemic racism *see* systemic racism; through psychology *see* racism, through psychology; *see also* antiracism/antiracist
Racism + Resilience + Resistance Integrative Study of Childhood Ecosystem (R³ISE) model 14, 33
racism, through psychology 26; antiracist professional identity, within psychology *see* antiracist professional identity, within psychology; context and relevance 32–33; critical consciousness 37–38; ecocultural theory and ethnotheories 34–35; empowerment 35–36; healing justice 41–42; partnering directly with impacted communities 43–45; problematization 42–43; psychological measures and assessments 39–41; psychological research 38–39; resilience 36–37
REAL (Recognize, Educate, Advocate, and Listen) 127–128
redefining success 74–75
reevaluating classroom norms 71
reflect and adapt 24, 82, 107
reflective practice 17, 27, 49, 103; for mentors 98; for teachers 68
reflect on potential barriers 24, 82, 107
relational skills 95
REM (racially and ethnically marginalized) communities in higher education 100
representation 26, 70, 75, 78–79, 87, 98, 113
RES *see* racial-ethnic political socialization (RES)
resilience 13, 14, 26, 36–38, 50, 82, 94–96, 99, 100, 103, 109, 121, 123
resistant capital 14
resource disparities 72
restorative circles 74, 123, 124
restorative practices 70, 72–74, 77–79, 83
RST *see* racial stress and trauma (RST)

Sacramento State: initiatives 104; policies, MMDLE 102–103
scaffold/scaffolding 2, 22, 25, 63, 89
scaffolded approach 25
school: policies 60, 61, 70–71, 73; traditions 75, 79
School Health Advisory Council (SHAC) 123–124
SDOH *see* social determinants of health (SDOH)
self-awareness 17, 20, 58, 59, 68, 121
self-critique 127
self-evaluation 127
sense of agency 80, 94–96, 99
SHAC *see* School Health Advisory Council (SHAC)
significant real-world consequences 7
silence 4, 12, 61, 69
situational analysis 25
Sloan, T. 45
social: capital 13–14; construction 7; identity development, workshops on 94; justice *see* social justice; stratification 15
social determinants of health (SDOH) 114–116, 120, 121, 132; and bioecological model 116–118; community 128
social justice 95; lens, leadership programs with 94–95; movements 91
socially constructed concept 7
societal taboo 61
Society for the Research on Child Development 32
socio-cultural: and antiracist context 116; and cross-cultural competence 49
sociohistorical context (MMDLE) 90, 91
sociopolitical development 37
sphere of influence 6
"stress hormone" 119
structural barriers 71, 73, 97
structural inequities 37, 68, 69, 100, 115
structural racism 6, 9, 14, 15, 100, 119; *see also* racism/racial
structured practice 80
students: action committee members 125; advocacy student (client)-driven programs 125; BIPOC 67; Black 67; (client)-driven programs 125; development, intersectionality and critical consciousness in 93–95; and

early-career professionals 1; identities 92–93; organization 106; post-traditional 87, 106; "student-centered" 59; voice 73–74, 77, 102–104
support groups, BWT 130
supportive structures 96
systemic context 60
systemic inequities 8, 18, 19, 21, 28, 70–74, 79, 83, 90, 93, 100, 123
systemic language 71
systemic perspectives in teaching practices 61
systemic racism 4, 7, 9, 96; negative effects of 14; pervasive impact of 6; *see also* racism/racial

teachers: to adapt based on feedback 68; critical reflection for 68; equity literacy for 70–71; positionality and racial literacy 79; racial literacy for 69–70; saviorism 60
teachers teach who they are 59, 62–63
teacher-student interaction 59
time, role of bioecological model 11, 12
TMER *see* Transconceptual Model of Empowerment and Resilience (TMER)
traditional: *vs.* antiracist teaching practices 76; classroom management techniques 72; educational goals 74; metrics 101
Traditional Zone of Proximal Development 63–65, *64*
Transconceptual Model of Empowerment and Resilience (TMER) 36–38

Understanding White supremacy as systemic 69
UDL *see* Universal Design for Learning (UDL)

United States: Department of Health and Human Services 130; foundation of 4; identity of 1; "post-traditional" 87; society 46
Universal Design for Learning (UDL) 77

visual representation, of MMDLE model 90
Vygotsky, L. 59; Zone of Proximal Development 26, 63–65, *64*

Walensky, R. P. 127
weathering 114, 118
Western, Educated, Industrialized, Rich, and Democratic societies (WEIRD) populations 38–39
White racial identity development 70
White teachers 66, 67, 69
White/Whiteness: cultural norms 67; mentors 98; peers 113; racial identity development 70; as "sign system" 65–67; teachers 67, 69; zones 67
White Zones of Proximal Development (WZPD) 65–67, *66*, 73, 81
Wood, L. 102–103
working parents 105
WZPD *see* White Zones of Proximal Development (WZPD)

xenophobia 117

Yosso, T. J. 13, 14; concept of navigational capital 98
Youth Risk Behavior Surveillance System 122

zero-tolerance policies 75
Zone of Proximal Development (Vygotsky) 26, 63–65, *64*

For Product Safety Concerns and Information please contact our EU
representative GPSR@taylorandfrancis.com
Taylor & Francis Verlag GmbH, Kaufingerstraße 24, 80331 München, Germany

www.ingramcontent.com/pod-product-compliance
Lightning Source LLC
Chambersburg PA
CBHW071821230426
43670CB00013B/2529